MANAGING CREATIVITY

MANAGING WORK AND ORGANIZATIONS SERIES

Edited by Dr Graeme Salaman, Professor of Organisation Studies at the Faculty of Social Sciences and the Open Business School, the Open University

Current titles:

Peter Anthony: *Managing Culture*
David Casey: *Managing Learning in Organizations*
Timothy Clark: *Managing Consultants*
Rohan Collier: *Combating Sexual Harassment in the Workplace*
Howard Davis and Richard Scase: *Managing Creativity*
Paul Iles: *Managing Staff Selection and Assessment*
Ian McLoughlin and Stephen Gourlay: *Enterprise Without Unions*
Graham Mole: *Managing Management Development*
Graeme Salaman: *Managing*
Jenny Shaw and Diane Perrons: *Making Gender Work*
Keith Sisson and John Storey: *The Realities of Human Resource Management*
John Storey and Keith Sisson: *Managing Human Resources and Industrial Relations*

MANAGING CREATIVITY

THE DYNAMICS OF WORK AND ORGANIZATION

Howard Davis and Richard Scase

Open University Press
Buckingham · Philadelphia

Open University Press
Celtic Court
22 Ballmoor
Buckingham
MK18 1XW

email: enquiries@openup.co.uk
world wide web: www.openup.co.uk

and
325 Chestnut Street
Philadelphia, PA 19106, USA

First Published 2000

A catalogue record of this book is available from the British Library

ISBN   0 335 20693 X (pb)   0 335 20694 8 (hb)

Library of Congress Cataloging-in-Publication Data Available

Typeset by Type Study, Scarborough
Printed in Great Britain by St Edmundsbury Press Ltd,
Bury St Edmunds, Suffolk

CONTENTS

Preface   vi

1 MANAGING THE CREATIVE PROCESS   1

2 THE CREATIVE INDUSTRIES   23

3 THE ORGANIZATION OF CREATIVE WORK   51

4 MANAGING CREATIVE ORGANIZATIONAL
   CULTURES   78

5 TRENDS IN CREATIVE ORGANIZATIONS   104

6 CREATIVE EMPLOYEES: THEIR ATTITUDES
   AND VALUES   129

7 THE CREATIVE CHALLENGE   150

Appendix: Research methods   170
References   173
Index   179

PREFACE

Readers will be familiar with the transformations that are occurring in the advanced economies of the world. As the production of manufactured goods shifts to China and the 'tiger' economies of South East Asia, the industrialized countries of Europe and the United States are becoming information- and science-based. The revolution in information and communications technologies is transforming these economies, their markets and the skills required of their labour forces. The same forces are leading to the restructuring of organizations and the methods by which they are managed. As part and parcel of these broader processes of change the creative industries, as they are now commonly called, have emerged as a significant economic as well as cultural force. Analysis and discussion of the organizational dynamics of these industries is the core concern of this book.

What are the characteristics of information societies and of the creative industries? Essentially, the concepts of information and creativity refer to the ways in which data, ideas or symbols become the predominant trading asset of organizations. Through the analysis and collection of data, companies are able to accumulate information which they are then able to use for the purposes of doing business. For example, a chain of supermarkets acquires information about its customers which it then uses to plan the purchase of particular products from manufacturers and suppliers. But also, with this information, it is able to market and retail its goods and services in distinctive and competitive ways. In a sense, supermarket chains are 'non-productive' and yet they promote services on the basis of detailed information. Similarly, manufacturers no longer make profits simply out of the tangible goods they produce. Indeed, production is often undertaken in other countries as part of a global supply chain. What makes manufacturers competitive is the information they collect and then analyse for the purposes of meeting customer requirements, the research and development function, sales and marketing strategies, and, of course, product innovation.

In an information society, a growing proportion of the labour force is engaged in the collection, analysis and interpretation of information. It expands into all areas of the economy ranging from retailing and manufacturing to financial services, public sector administration, health care and welfare, education and entertainment. Service economies therefore require different skills compared to those needed in manufacturing. There is, of course, a continuing requirement for occupations involving repetitive, routine tasks. Working as a checkout assistant in a supermarket – a modern service occupation – offers no greater opportunities for personal growth than being an unskilled operative on a factory production line. Being employed in a telesales call centre is no more personally enriching than packing products in a warehouse. But alongside these jobs, there are many that require the exercise of intellectual and creative skills. They increase in both numbers and importance with the growth of the information society. This increasing proportion of the labour force is expected to have two major attributes. The first is the intellectual skills to analyse and process data. This needs expertise in information technology and the ability to manage information systems appropriately. But second, and probably more important, is the ability to 'visualize' in order to develop new products and services. The asset involved here is the ability to 'think the unthinkable', to be 'original', to work 'creatively'.

In manufacturing organizations, creativity is incorporated either within traditional craft skills or institutionalized in terms of what is often described as the 'research and development' function. It is organized as a service or support function. Career paths are usually restricted, reward systems less favourable, and the status of research and development workers lower, than for general managers. In other words, those responsible for the 'creation' of new products and services – upon which the longer term survival of the business depends – are often less valued. But in a service economy, where the key assets of businesses are the collection, analysis and interpretation of information, the management of creativity becomes a major organizational challenge.

Most large manufacturing and administrative companies are organized according to the principles of hierarchical line management. Activities are systematically controlled through a precisely delineated division of labour and formal reporting mechanisms. Work processes are highly routinized through protocols and procedures which stipulate how tasks should be executed. The management of creativity requires different processes of organization. These stem from the values of creative workers and their expectations of how they should be allowed to perform their tasks. Essentially, creativity is about experimentation and innovation, leading to the development of new products and services. Employees who, because of their education and biographical experiences, 'think creatively' will be inclined to resent control and being 'told what to do'. How, then, can they be managed if large organizations are not to be chaotic?

Often there will be organizational tensions but these have to be accommodated if creativity is to be utilized for organizational purposes. In general, employees express creativity in ways which contrast sharply with formal models of organization. They value their personal autonomy (independence), behave in nonconformist ways (displaying divergent thinking, unorthodox ways of doing things) and thrive on indeterminacy (the ambiguities, unpredictability and the uncertainties associated with the exploration and the implementation of their creative ideas). Each of these characteristics is in sharp contrast to conventional management assumptions about what should constitute the guiding principles of efficient organization. How then do companies structure their work processes to incorporate employee autonomy and creativity, while at the same time ensuring control and coordination? This is the question tackled in this book. What will emerge is an answer suggesting that there are a variety of organizational responses, each different in the way it attempts to resolve the tensions associated with the management of creativity.

How is the management of creativity to be researched? In this study, the method is to focus on organizations that may be regarded as 'critical cases', meaning those which unavoidably, or in extreme ways, manifest the tensions and the structural accommodations associated with the management of creativity. Organizations in the media and creative industries are therefore the main centre of attention. The focus is upon television and radio broadcasting, the performing arts, advertising, recorded music and book publishing. This is a diverse range of activities and in no way can it be regarded as representative of broader patterns either within other creative industries or more generally. But having said that, it is our belief that the trends occurring in these industries are indicative of wider organizational patterns relating to the management of creativity. A further question is: what should replace the management principles and practices inherited from industrial society in the organizations which predominate in post-industrial society? This book aims to present some of the evidence upon which an understanding of those principles might be developed. Therefore, we have avoided the conventions of a pure research monograph and have chosen a style designed to make the arguments and research evidence accessible to a wide and multidisciplinary audience. Among this audience, we hope, will be practitioners in the creative industries, as well as students and researchers with an interest in the study of organizations.

As with all research, many acknowledgements are due because without the cooperation of a number of people and organizations, this particular study would not have been possible. The Economic and Social Research Council funded the research. This allowed Philippa Summersby to be engaged as a Research Fellow at the University of Kent to conduct the detailed case studies and a large proportion of the interviews. She contributed substantially to the empirical foundations of the study. Christine Daymon provided additional help with the interviews and constant encouragement. Special thanks are also due to the senior managers of all those organizations that allowed their operating processes to be observed as well as those individuals who allowed themselves to be interviewed, often in very demanding and hectic circumstances. The writing up of this study partly took place while Richard Scase was visiting professor at the Institute for Social and Economic Research at the University of Essex. He is grateful to the Director, Professor Jonathan Gershuny, and his colleagues for their enthusiastic help and encouragement. Library staff at the European University Institute, Florence gave generous assistance to Howard Davis during his stay under the EUSSIRF scheme. This is also gratefully acknowledged. Writing was also undertaken in a small village in northern Sweden. This was a source of local curiosity as well as both psychological and material support. Anni Elving should be singled out for particular mention, not least for the excellence of her (quite voluntary and insistent) cooking. As always, all weaknesses in this study are entirely the responsibility of the authors.

MANAGING THE CREATIVE PROCESS

Recent patterns of organizational change have brought the issue of creativity to the foreground of management theory and practice. It has not always occupied such a significant place. Management ideas were first formulated as general principles when industrialization was reaching its peak, at a time when disorder, conflict and lack of control were seen as the main threats to organizational health. Today, in contrast, lack of flexibility and over-control are perceived as an equal danger. This chapter identifies the reasons for this fundamental shift in the framework of management and sets out a number of key characteristics of the work process in the context of creative industries and, more generally, the information age. In a post-industrial society, the core of economic activity ceases to be organized around manufacturing and the production of capital goods. Instead of the factory and the assembly line, the office and the computer become the pivotal centres of economic life. The human labour required in these new places of work is no longer associated with the execution of routine manual skills but, instead, demands the use of different kinds of mental or intellectual abilities. This is not to say that in a post-industrial society routine tasks are abolished. Far from it, as is witnessed by the continuation of low-paid jobs in the rapidly expanding service sectors of retailing, catering and those jobs providing different kinds of personal services. Indeed, the emergence of the so-called information society is also creating many new poorly rewarded and routine jobs in call centres, data processing and various information gathering activities in different sectors of the economy. But what is distinctive about post-industrial development is the emergence of categories of occupations in which the exercise of personal creativity and complex intellectual skills are their distinguishing features.[1] Of course, such abilities were also needed in industrial society but even so, their relevance is now much more pronounced. Witness the rapid growth of institutions of higher education to provide graduates with the skills to meet this need.

Although these jobs are not yet numerically dominant in post-industrial society, their contribution to economic activity is very significant. Those with the relevant intellectual and creative skills are now often the basis of a company's competitive position since it is the design, development, marketing and selling of products and services rather than their manufacture which are at the core of the business. The latter can now be done more cheaply in the newly industrialized areas of South East Asia and China. What this means is that the structuring of organizations and how they are managed reflect this change. To manage and to organize the work processes of those who constitute intellectual and creative labour it is necessary to apply different assumptions, methodologies and principles of organizational behaviour to those used when monitoring the tasks of factory workers, concentrated in large, single locations. Hence the management of creativity becomes a key organizational issue. This chapter examines these processes, and particularly the tensions and conflicts associated with them. One of the core arguments of what follows is that the search for solutions to these problems has a profound impact on the design of organizations, their social relationships and their styles of management.

'Management' and 'creativity' are often seen as contradictory terms. To an extent, this reflects a commonly held view that to be creative, it is necessary to be independent from the control of others. It is not surprising that 'freelance' is frequently associated with the artists, writers, researchers, and others who work beyond the confines of the employment relationship. In other words, freedom is seen as a necessary prerequisite for creativity because such activity can never be precisely defined and measured. Indeed, it is often claimed that creative freedom requires 'authenticity' – a capacity for self-expression – that is unlikely to be realized in most conventional organizational settings. Management, by contrast, is usually regarded as a mechanism of control, whereby diverse activities are coordinated for the purposes of achieving goals. In other words, organizations – as mechanisms of coordination – consist of control relationships whereby managers seek to impose direction upon action and behaviour. Such mechanisms inevitably restrict the capacity for individual choice, free expression and authentic creativity; certainly by comparison with those working freelance.

The theory and practice of management generally alleges that to participate in work organizations it is necessary for individuals to comply with a variety of structural and cultural constraints. There is the acceptance that organizational rules and authority relations can inhibit innovation and creativity. This has led to alternative ideas and theories designed to increase the flexibility and dynamism of the organization. One of the earliest developments in modern organizational theory was the attempt to use informal social organization to increase employee morale and motivation (Mayo, 1975). The emphasis on 'teamwork' is another such attempt, along with the 'art of Japanese management' which was until recently in vogue in western economies. However, these alternatives can actually diminish the capacity for individual and group creative expression. The emphasis on 'mission statements', formally prescribed aims and objectives, teamwork and shared cultural values can also have a similar outcome. This demonstrates that the contra-positioning of 'management' and 'creativity' is flawed because the polarization relies on misplaced and rather simplistic assumptions. It treats 'management' as a homogeneous principle of organizational reality, failing to do justice to the diversity of forms of organization as well as styles of managerial control (Morgan, 1986). Equally, the concept of 'creativity' has little descriptive or analytical value unless it is given some degree of operational specificity so that it can be used for organizational analysis. Typically, discussions of management and creativity generate rhetorical appeals rather than analytical categories that encourage empirical enquiry into specific organizational processes. Those engaged in creative activity often complain of 'managerialism' when asked to be more accountable for their 'outputs' and how these may be achieved, while 'management' often objects when creative employees claim that their expertise is not readily subject to 'rational' criteria of organizational performance. Undoubtedly, in any organization there are tensions between those who exercise managerial control on the one hand and others who are subject to their dictates. This is particularly evident in the case of employees who, by virtue of their biographical experiences, such as higher education in the arts and humanities, have internalized expectations about job autonomy and the need for work to offer them opportunities for personal growth, self-enrichment and the capacity for personal 'creativity'.

Traditionally, within the context of manufacturing society, such groups constituted a small proportion of the labour force. However, as a result of changes which have occurred in the structure of modern economies – the shift towards service occupations in a post-industrial, 'information' society – their cultural and economic significance has grown. Accordingly, management processes and the design of organizations have had to adapt in order to respond to the changing work expectations of the growing numbers of knowledge-based employees (Brown and Scase, 1994). Before specifying some of these trends in more detail, it is useful to present the background in terms of the main characteristics of traditional management paradigms. It will then be possible to highlight and contrast the changes in management processes which are most typical of the emerging sectors of the economy – such as the creative industries.

Management and bureaucracy

It was Max Weber in *Economy and Society* (1978) who, in a systematic manner, first summarized the essential features of bureaucratic forms of organization and the explicit mechanisms of managerial control that are inherent within them. He regarded their operational precision, discipline and reliability as the clearest articulation of rational tendencies within modern capitalist economies.

Essential to his characterization of the 'ideal type' administrative bureaucracy are a number of themes, the most important being the following. First, there is the emphasis on specialization, according to which the work of individuals is broken down into distinct and routine duties. Second, there is a tendency to formalism, whereby rules and procedures are given superordinate authority. There is little scope for personal discretion and interpretation. This leads to standardization and, therefore, control over the behaviour of all participating members. Third, such control is exercised through hierarchy, in terms of which a 'pyramid' of authority clearly defines how each level supervises the others beneath it. Fourth, reward systems, such as payments and promotion, are established according to universalistic and explicit criteria which, in turn, encourage employee compliance to the organization's procedures and goals. Fifth, there is the offer of career tenure to jobholders who are assured of employment so long as they adhere to the stipulated procedures and practices of the organization. This is a further criterion that controls behaviour and reinforces prevailing organizational norms and practices.

Until at least the late 1970s, the prevailing paradigm of management and organization design emphasized the need for forms of bureaucratic control. A more recent generation of management thinkers has popularized the notions of change, flexibility and freedom from the shackles of bureaucracy (Kanter, 1983; Peters, 1987). At the same time, organizational theorists have tried to come to terms with trends that are difficult to explain within the Weberian framework of rationalization (Clegg, 1990; Hassard and Parker, 1993; Ray and Reed, 1994). However, the fundamental assumption in management practice has been that behaviour can be managed on a rational basis and, accordingly, that rational operating structures should determine the design of profit-making organizations. This principle is expressed through the imposition of a detailed division of labour and concomitant rules and procedures. Originally, such principles evolved out of the study of work organization in manufacturing processes. Scientific management (Taylor, 1972) and Fordism became the underlying principles according to which managers exercised tight supervisory control over shop floor employees. However, it was not long before such principles were seen to be appropriate for application to all spheres of work. These included managerial as well as non-managerial jobs in most sectors of the economy. Hence, the principles of scientific management were rapidly adopted as the most appropriate means for the rational control of work. In the first instance these were applied to manufacturing organizations and then to administrative systems. Today, the implementation of these principles is found in all spheres of economic and social activity; from retailing to education and leisure and recreation services. There is, indeed, what may be described as the progressive rationalization or 'McDonaldization' of everyday life (Ritzer, 1993).

The outcome of the application of these principles has been a theory of organization design which is synonymous with the notion of bureaucracy. This incorporates a number of core features. Employee conformity and compliance is obtained through the use of centralized control mechanisms based upon hierarchical decision making. Communication processes are vertically structured so that those with managerial authority monitor and control flows of information and determine the allocation of resources. The paradigm emphasizes the need for tasks to be allocated according to strictly defined criteria of superordination and subordination. Organizational values emphasize compliance and, as a result, the need to foster what has often been termed the 'bureaucratic personality'. Thus, organizational participants are discouraged from exercising initiative, and from being creative and developing individual strategies for achieving organizational goals. Instead, they are expected to undertake their tasks according to clearly defined criteria. The total work process is broken down into a precisely delineated division of labour within which specialization is encouraged. There is a preponderance of accountable and measurable routine tasks and a minimum of creative, innovative activity. Actors are interdependent and the failure to comply with procedures only creates organizational confusion. 'Predictability', 'routinization', 'measurement' and 'accountability' are the essential features of bureaucratic organizations. Hence, these underlying principles are considered to be no less pertinent for determining the rational allocation of duties among managers, professionals and technical experts than for those undertaking lower grade administrative tasks and manual work.

For bureaucratic organizations to function effectively, it is also necessary for them to nurture cultures that are appropriate to such structures. Role cultures tend to be pronounced, reinforcing conformity of behaviour of the kind mentioned above and according to which the bureaucracy is predisposed to undertake tasks in a 'satisfactory' as distinct from an 'optimum' or innovative manner. Equally, employee recruitment will tend to focus upon those who can demonstrate the ability to conform, to learn the rules of the game, who are prepared to be compliant within hierarchically structured roles of superordination and subordination, and who are able to cooperate with others within a functionally interdependent division of labour. They are not encouraged to be creative, entrepreneurial or individualist, since such patterns of behaviour – as variously interpreted within particular organizational settings – can be seen as potentially deviant, leading to the undermining of bureaucratic cultures.

Assumptions about the appropriateness of such forms of bureaucratic organization persist in large sectors of the modern economy despite forces that are rendering them less relevant. In education, health and welfare, for example, there are strong pressures towards more bureaucracy. Professional and skilled employees find their autonomy in work being eroded as they become subject to tighter controls. The organizational attributes discussed above remain pronounced within present-day assumptions of 'managerialism'. In other words, the principles of modern management continue to be equated with the control mechanisms traditionally associated with bureaucracy. These, however, fail to recognize that it is but *one* type of management process (Goffee and Scase, 1995). With bureaucracy's emphasis upon control and imposed conformity, it is understandable why 'management' should be seen as the antithesis of innovation and of work settings which are conducive to the expression of individual 'creativity'.

Organizational change

Such assumptions ignore the extent to which, in all sectors of the economy and especially within the creative industries, bureaucratic forms of organization are being challenged or reassessed. In the 1990s, many companies came to recognize the economic, cultural and psychological costs associated with these structures. Profit-making corporations are no longer able to be competitive if they retain hierarchies of managers located within centralized administrative processes. Hence, 'downsizing' and the flattening of organizational structures have become managerial priorities. The rapid industrialization of South East Asian economies has also generated greater competitive pressures for business organizations in Europe and the United States with the result that corporate leaders have been compelled to reassess their business practices and their assumptions that Fordist and bureaucratic-based management systems are the most effective. This has led not only to the rapid restructuring and redesign of many organizations but a fundamental change in managers' expectations of the performance of employees. 'Creativity', 'innovation' and 'risk' are encouraged instead of compliance and conformity (Morgan, 1989). Flexibility and informality are valued in preference to formality. With this, employees are expected to be psychologically immersed in their jobs – rather than simply to fulfil role prescriptions as specified within bureaucracies. It is for this reason that senior managers devote so much attention to corporate 'culture building' since by this they attempt to obtain psychological commitment rather than gaining compliance through employee adherence to explicitly stated rules and procedures.[2] This, however, can give rise to an interesting paradox because such strategies for obtaining employee commitment may be counterproductive to those necessary for nurturing employee independence and creativity. Thus, an almost compulsive emphasis upon core corporate values and norms can inhibit individuality and self-expression and, hence, creativity.

The basic principles upon which large-scale organizations have been established, then, are undergoing fundamental reappraisal. Even assumptions about economies of scale are now regarded as less valid. There has been a return to the alleged virtues of small business and of other small-scale units of organization. Contemporary management theorists often extol the need for a thriving small business sector on the grounds that small and medium-sized enterprises are more efficient than their larger counterparts (Goss, 1991). This can be a result of the tighter forms of managerial control that can be exercised in small firms. Even so, it is argued that within these it is possible to develop harmonious employer–staff relations. Consequently, employee motivation will be high and so, too, will commitment to the business. Further, it is argued that there are greater opportunities for encouraging employee creativity directly because of the absence of formalized control mechanisms and demarcated managerial roles. These benefits can be reinforced by developing patterns of ownership based upon partnerships and by employee participation in profit-sharing schemes.

In a similar fashion, within large organizations, a re-evaluation of the economies of scale has led many to restructure on the basis of devolved but directly accountable operating units. Within these, there are attempts to recreate the cultures of classical small-scale entrepreneurial enterprises that compel employees to be more responsive to changing market requirements. In the absence of formalized hierarchical structures that offer long-term career progression, employees are rewarded on the basis of short-term performance and incentive systems. They are offered fixed-term contracts and given performance targets against which they are measured. Within the context of small-scale operating units and their associated 'flattened' structures, the nature of interpersonal relations and quality of management style is different. Instead of an emphasis upon formalism and impersonal procedures, the attempt is made to cultivate informal, personal and team relations based upon face-to-face interaction. Such devolved operating units are integrated through mechanisms that avoid the use of bureaucratic forms of hierarchical control. The use of managerial and supervisory hierarchies, whose prime function is to integrate and coordinate activities, is being superseded by information systems whereby performance of the separate operating units is measured on a regular, even hourly basis. Developments in information technology are rendering redundant the need for geographical centralization. Instead, employees – even those working within the same operating units – may be dispersed on a regional, national and international basis. It is for such reasons that many modern corporations are described as enterprise webs (Reich, 1992), sites of reflexive production (Lash and Urry, 1994) or networks (Castells, 1996). Processes of internal restructuring have been reinforced by the fact that many 'in-house' activities are now 'out-sourced' to various sub-contractors. As a result, many organizational boundaries are now weakly defined, with a key responsibility of management being to coordinate and interface with different external agencies for the provision of products and services. Not only do such organizational networks have to be established, but also continually maintained and adapted (Chattell, 1998).

In this discussion of organizational change, a number of key factors have been emphasized. The need for businesses to be more cost-effective and competitive by having lower overheads has been a major force behind processes of debureaucratization. Labour and production processes are more decentralized. At the same time, the increasing pressure of global market competition has compelled organizations to be more responsive to the needs of customers. No longer can they assume that markets are stable, or that the demand for their products and services will be reasonably predictable. Product life cycles have shortened and profit margins declined in many economic sectors. Customers, whether they are manufacturers or consumers of finished goods, are more demanding in their requirements, forcing businesses to be more responsive to their needs. The result may be that strategic management, planning and financial control become tighter and more centralized. But just as important as a force bringing about organizational transformation is the changing structure of the world economy and, associated with this, the transformation of the labour force. This, in turn, has affected expectations and experiences of work as well as rewards and working relationships.

Economic restructuring

Most countries have restructured their economies over the recent decades. Changes which have occurred in Britain have been among the most rapid and far reaching. For instance, employment in manufacturing as a proportion of the total labour force declined from 34 per cent in 1971 to less than 18 per cent in 1998, and to 17 per cent in the year 2000. By contrast, service sector occupations, in areas such as business services, retailing, distribution, administrative processes, entertainment and leisure, increased from 12 per cent in 1971 to 23 per cent in 1995, with a further 2 per cent increase to the year 2000 (Institute for Employment Research, 1998). Such structural shifts have had ramifications for the nature of employment relations and conditions of work which the statistics themselves fail to disclose. The decline in manufacturing, for example, has led to a rapid reduction in the demand for manual work.

While the percentage of semi-skilled and skilled machine operators declined by approximately 50 per cent between 1971 and 1991, and those engaged in sales and clerical and secretarial services remained roughly the same, the percentage of those working in managerial, professional and technical positions increased dramatically. The number of managers and administrators grew by 50 per cent during the twenty-year period. But the most dramatic expansion is in professional and technical occupations, that is, those who possess intellectual capital of one kind or another which they either sell to employers in increasingly global labour markets or use as the basis for setting up their own businesses or for trading as self-employed. These have more than doubled as a percentage of the labour force and in 1991 accounted for one in five of all those employed. In the year 2000 they constitute approximately 25 per cent of the gainfully employed. A significant proportion of this group is self-employed professionals who sell their services to others in the market place. As a category, the self-employed had grown to 13 per cent of the labour force in 1991 compared with 8 per cent twenty years earlier. If, traditionally, the self-employed have typically been providers of low-skill services – often drawing upon manual or craft skills of one kind or another – they are now likely to be trading with various specialist, technical, expert, professional and creative skills. Such competences are sometimes offered in-house on a relatively long-term basis, while they may also be offered to a broader range of clients on negotiated shorter term contractual relationships.

Associated with these changes has been the demise of forms of management control already discussed. If the principles of scientific management emerged as a mechanism to measure and control behaviour first in the factories and then in other spheres of employment activity, they have now become less significant. The shift away from manufacturing has entailed a move from large-scale units of 'mass' production to smaller workplaces where relationships are more personal and face-to-face. Equally, the growth of professional and information-based occupations is leading to the development of post-bureaucratic methods of managerial control (Goffee and Scase, 1995).

The sociology of organizations has tended to emphasize how management, in a relatively unfettered way, can impose working practices and controls upon their employees. The enduring influence of the systems or functionalist paradigm (Burrell and Morgan, 1979) means that it has difficulty conceding that managers are usually compelled to adjust to the actions of their staff and to negotiate appropriate working practices and relationships. Indeed, sociologists have tended to focus upon practices in large manufacturing organizations and within the context of class theory, to emphasize the 'industrial divide' and associated conflict between management and workers. They have focused upon the imposition of management controls and sources of workers' resistance to these. Finding an explanation for this was the preoccupation of sociologists in the 1970s and early 1980s. The ideas were best exemplified by Braverman who, in his book *Labor and Monopoly Capital* (1974), argued that the principles of scientific management, Fordism and bureaucratic modes of control were virtually the only management tools for increasing worker productivity.

Creative industries

As a consequence of their preoccupation with manufacturing and conflict theories, sociologists and organizational theorists have devoted less attention to other forms of organization. Despite a growing interest in the sociology of leisure, entertainment and the mass media, little research has focused upon work processes and organizational structures in these sectors (Ettema and Whitney, 1982). As far as the creative industries are concerned, the emphasis has tended to be upon newspapers and television. The focus has been upon three key issues. First, those of ownership and control – studies, for example, of cross-ownership and how far this constitutes a threat to popular participation and open debate in a liberal democracy (Garnham, 1990; Murdock, 1990). The second emphasis has been upon the manufacture and dissemination of news and information as means of cultural domination by the media. The third focus has been on the relationship between media messages and public opinion. Thus, the analysis of media companies from the perspective of work and organization has been generally neglected. If the media industries have been studied mainly from the perspective of political economy or of cultural studies this is even more true of the creative industries in general, which include a wide range of cultural production apart from the traditional core of broadcasting and publishing. There is a fuller description of these approaches and the structure of the creative industries in Chapter 2. However, viewed primarily as organizations, what is particularly significant about them is the extent to which managerially imposed control mechanisms cannot be taken for granted, certainly by comparison with those in large manufacturing industries. There are a number of reasons for this.

There is an almost indeterminate feel to management within these organizations. There are, of course, exceptions – as will be illustrated later – but, in comparison with most large-scale industrial corporations, creative companies have a less clearly defined hierarchical management structure. Relatively speaking, job roles are loosely defined and reporting mechanisms often lack the clarity which they have in manufacturing companies. Furthermore, and equally important for employee motivation, managerial identities are underplayed. Certainly, there is a management function which – as stipulated in any definition of its core task – is primarily concerned with controlling and coordinating the behaviour of others for the purposes of achieving goals. In manufacturing organizations, this function is explicitly executed by cadres of managers who derive their organizational identities from undertaking this task. The major intention of scientific management is both to clarify and to systematize these duties and responsibilities according to universal rational principles. In most creative industry organizations, by contrast, the management function is typically integrated within the professional, expert and creative roles of those who would neither regard themselves, nor would be perceived by others, primarily as managers. Instead of managing through mechanisms of formal hierarchical control and divisions of labour, there is a greater tendency for the management of core work processes to be exercised through mechanisms of mutual adjustment. According to this, interpersonal negotiation and patterns of mutual reciprocity tend to shape the execution of tasks and the definition of organizational goals in relation to specific circumstances and conditions. In short, it is hardly an exaggeration to say that creative companies are predisposed to structuring work processes in ways that reduce the need for formal managerial control. Obviously, there are corporate executives responsible for strategic issues as well as for safeguarding the interests of shareholders and these may, indeed, be viewed by employees as senior management. But below this strategic apex, and in terms of day-to-day operational activities, the execution of most core production tasks is undertaken through a process of self-managed 'mutual adjustment' (Mintzberg, 1983). Hence, this is often according to practices that would be regarded as problematic according to many of the criteria of scientific management and which, if only for this reason, may sometimes be perceived as inefficient.

Work processes based on mutual adjustment

But why should processes of mutual adjustment be so pronounced to the extent that traditional forms of bureaucratic management are often viewed as inappropriate within the creative industries? Primarily, it is because of the nature of their output. Unlike large-scale, assembly line manufacturing – which was the original paradigm case for theories of organization – the production of cultural goods and services can rarely be standardized on a long-term basis. For example, as genres develop there may be print runs of books, or television and radio programming, according to formats which – based upon detailed audience and market research – lead to predictable scheduling. But even so, such shifts towards standardization operate within the context of work processes organized around 'one-off' and short-run projects. Change is more rapid and there is a greater degree of unpredictability and risk. Hence, the indeterminate nature of work tasks encourages mutual adjustment as the key organizational principle. This is reinforced by the nature of the markets of most privately owned creative companies which are usually subject to fluctuations in their audiences' tastes and fashion. Customer demand for their products is very uncertain in comparison with the market for many durable products – and, as a result, there are severe structural constraints on the extent to which work processes can be standardized and determined by hierarchical methods of management.

Accordingly, it is necessary for creative companies continuously to adapt and redefine their activities. This will often lead to the need to focus upon particular types of production and genre. For example, publishers will specialize in particular types of fiction or non-fiction. Television production companies develop skills for producing certain kinds of drama, entertainment series or documentary programmes. Theatre production companies will also specialize in one tradition or another. Such forces leading towards product specialization are an outcome of the need to innovate, change and adapt in order to survive. Indeed, this may generate contradictions for many media companies; forces to innovate that lead to product specialization can, in turn, be conducive to standardization which may inhibit innovation and, hence, longer term company performance. Of these two tendencies, the culture of innovation is likely to be the more pronounced. This is why work processes organized around the principle of mutual adjustment prevail since, in this way, companies can be responsive to changing demands in the market place. Mutual adjustment is a means of coordinating inputs within the work process from those with a wide variety of talents and skills. Organized around projects, these elements are constantly reconstituted so that the organization can be adaptive and, therefore, innovative. Accordingly, formally prescribed hierarchical control mechanisms cannot be imposed. Standardized rules and procedures would introduce rigidities and an inappropriate division of labour which would inhibit collaborative, project-driven work processes.

A further factor inhibiting the application of formalized, bureaucratic management techniques is in relation to the nature of the skills that constitute the operating core of media companies.

Despite the diversity of talents and skills found in media organizations, they share a number of common features that do not lend themselves to routinization and formalized mechanisms of bureaucratic control. The skills exercised are often indeterminate and cannot be precisely defined, described and measured. There may be job descriptions and organizational charts describing roles and responsibilities but these often constitute little more than the formal representation of the way in which tasks are supposed to be executed as distinct from how they are actually undertaken. The level of general education is high with employees having invested heavily in developing their competence and varied skills. Even so, such education and training only provides such employees with the potential or capacity to undertake specific tasks. It is only by working with others through project-orientated processes of mutual adjustment that such general capacity is converted into technical abilities that are relevant for executing specific work tasks. This leads to interdependencies between colleagues who are then only able to exercise their own particular skills within an informally constituted and flexible division of labour. Accordingly, the nature of interpersonal relations can be as significant as technical expertise in shaping the composition of project teams and how they execute their tasks. Such mechanisms do not lend themselves to formalised hierarchies of control and it is usually necessary for senior staff to devolve responsibilities to employees. Mutual adjustment allows indeterminate human resources to be focused, converted and combined for the purpose of producing complex cultural products. This is particularly evident in those sectors of the creative industries where work processes are organized on the basis of projects, as in the case of theatre, film and television, and recorded music.

Within the creative industries, the indeterminacy of employee skills is often understood in terms of their 'personal creativity'. It is this, more than anything else, which inhibits the development of formalized management mechanisms according to which work tasks can be precisely defined and tightly controlled. Personal creative abilities are difficult to bureaucratize and are highly resistant to managerial attempts to 'deskill'. If, as Braverman (1974) proposed, the development of modern industry is characterized by transformation in the nature and organization of work, such that the all-round skills of craft workers have been subdivided into specific tasks that can then be executed according to routine procedures by deskilled employees, this is difficult to achieve with the work of creative employees. As such, there are limits to the extent to which the principles of scientific management – which are closely associated with such deskilling processes – can be applied. However, this is not to say that creative employees have always been able to resist managerial attempts to fragment and to deskill their work. Usually, it is in the interest of management to pursue such a strategy since the indeterminate nature of such work constitutes what are perceived to be sources of organizational uncertainty. If employees are able to manage these spheres, it gives them organizational power and, hence, a key bargaining resource (Crozier, 1964). There are many areas of work within the creative industries where senior managers have been able to break the control of employees over certain work activities and to impose routinized procedures. Developments in production and information technologies have sometimes enabled this to occur so that fewer creative skills are required (Francis, 1986; Legge *et al.*, 1991). But also, in conjunction with this, it has been possible to reduce the bargaining capacity of professional associations and trade unions which in the past have enabled creative employees to retain their control over key areas of work. In such circumstances, there are often conflicts and tensions to be witnessed in the processes of organizational restructuring. These have occurred not only in the media and creative sectors, both public and private, but also in professionally based institutions such as hospitals, schools, universities and research establishments.

The study of creativity

Developments in the creative industries therefore constitute a critical case within which these processes can be observed. There are constant negotiations and struggles over the organization of the creative process, the outcome of which is reflected in the great diversity of organizational forms. As already stated, there is no single paradigm of management which fully satisfies the criteria of universality and objectivity. Methods of bureaucratic control are but one of a number of managerial processes that are to be found (Morgan, 1986; Du Gay, 1996). In fact, there is a wide range of organizational settings in which the skills and tasks of employees not only constitute an important source of resistance to formalized managerial control but also, in a more explicit manner, determine the very nature of these management processes. The creative industries epitomize many of the organizational forms and practices associated with the contest over the control of indeterminacy and creativity. But what is creativity? How is it to be defined for the purposes of empirical enquiry?

There is, of course, a considerable literature on creativity including such classic studies as Koestler's (1964) which attempt to describe the conditions that give rise to the creative achievements of artists and scientists. There is much within social psychology as well as educational or management studies that shows how creativity is embedded in ordinary psychological and social processes. Whereas the former is inclined to focus upon attributes of the 'creative personality' or creative intelligence (Boden, 1990), the latter tends to discuss the practical measures whereby creativity – however it may be defined – can be nurtured within various work settings (Maslow, 1962; Morgan, 1989). Other discussions of organizational creativity are associated with the issue of how to manage product or process innovation (Twiss, 1986; Henry and Walker, 1991; Burns and Stalker, 1994). They often argue that it is difficult to be prescriptive although the management challenge is to create forms of organization design that nurture both individual creativity and corporate innovation and change. Despite the reliance on creativity activity for the constant generation of new products for the market, there has been little analysis of the work processes involved in the creative industries. Indeed, where they do exist, discussions of creative work by management theorists, as well as their more research-orientated social psychology colleagues, offer little help. The former group rarely defines what is meant by creativity while the latter tends to be preoccupied with identifying personality traits. Moreover, few sociologists, perhaps because of their preoccupation with manufacturing and administrative organizations, have addressed the matter although the concept of creativity has a central place in some general theories of social action (Joas, 1996).

Defining organizational creativity

From the perspective of organizational leaders applying the methods of scientific management, creative workers can be a source of organizational tension. As Winston Fletcher, a leading figure in advertising, remarks, creative people 'tend to be insecure, egotistical, stubborn, rebellious, poor timekeeping perfectionists who seek fame' (Fletcher, 1990). Similarly, according to Rogers' influential psychological theory, creativity is a process which grows out of the uniqueness of the individuals and their responses to circumstances. It involves 'independence of judgement, freedom of expression, novelty of construction and insight, openness to experience, freedom from petty restraints and inhibitions, an aesthetic sensitivity and cognitive flexibility' (Rogers, 1961). In other words, from a managerial point of view, creativity can be equated with individualism, eccentricity and even being unmanageable. Independence and nonconformity appear to characterize the creative person and the creative process. Therefore, in order for new ideas to be nurtured and for these to be translated into new products and services, it is necessary for organizations to develop structures and cultures that encourage rather than inhibit the autonomy and the nonconformity necessary for creative activity. This is particularly the case in the creative industries – just as it is in scientific research establishments and other expert-based businesses (for example, high-technology and pharmaceutical companies) – where corporate performance is dependent upon constant product innovation. Consequently, creativity needs to be viewed as a social process as much as a psychological phenomenon. It can be used to describe particular organizational processes or activities that are orientated to harnessing the creative talents of individuals to the innovative needs of their employing organizations. Such processes are characterized by at least three key features which relate to organizational forms rather than to traits of individual personality or behaviour. In conventional theories of organization they would be described as aspects of structure (division of labour, roles), culture (norms) and the work process (performance). In creative organizations these static concepts have to be given a more open and fluid meaning.

The first feature of the creative process in organizations is

19

autonomy, in that individuals occupy broadly defined work roles which allow them to experiment and to exercise relatively independent judgement in how they execute their tasks and fulfil organizational objectives. As a result, processes of mutual adjustment whereby semi-autonomous individuals constantly regroup according to the project at hand will be a pronounced feature of creative organizations. Little emphasis will be given to hierarchical and formally prescribed reporting mechanisms, since it will be recognized that employees require autonomy in the extent to which they can determine the nature of their working if they are to achieve organizational aims and objectives. Structures will be established that delineate spheres of operational autonomy.

The second feature of the creative organizational process is a culture of *nonconformity* in the way that tasks are executed. By contrast with the formally prescribed features of the bureaucratic organization that foster conformity and stifle innovation, creative work processes explicitly encourage employees to undertake their tasks and to pursue their goals in often different and unusual ways. There is a culture of nonconformity, often with an assumption that employees will behave in individualistic, non-standard, and even eccentric ways. Such an emphasis upon nonconformity is often expressed in organizations through vaguely defined patterns of work, relaxed dress codes and informal patterns of personal relations and communication. While the bureaucratic form of organization encourages conformity and submerges the personality to organizational practices and procedures, creative work processes emphasize individuality and personal difference. Nonconformity, then, becomes a predominant cultural attribute of such organizations.

A third feature of the creative process is *indeterminacy*. This refers to the extent to which employees not only enjoy relative independence or autonomy but how the achievement of organizational goals is translated into operational practices. While senior managers are responsible for setting overall strategic goals they are dependent upon an indeterminate creative work process for their interpretation and implementation. Indeed, in many work settings, the goals of the organization will be shaped by the creative work process, with senior managers having an almost entirely supportive or facilitative function. Many research institutes, software companies, medical establishments and, particularly, media companies operate in this way. The creative work process, which depends upon the interactions of relatively autonomous employees, determines the management process rather than vice versa. Hence, organizational strategies may be described as emergent rather than top-down and directive as in bureaucratic forms.

These, then, are the three key dimensions of creativity as an organizational process: *autonomy*, *nonconformity* and *indeterminacy*. The ways in which they are articulated will vary in different work settings. Within the creative industries, there are contrasts in organizational forms both within and between different sectors. For example, radio stations are structured differently from television companies; the recorded music industry contains a wide variety of organizational forms, some of which are more bureaucratic than others. But, irrespective of such differences, all sectors – to varying degrees – incorporate a creative organizational process. Autonomy, nonconformity and indeterminacy are common features that have to be addressed. The outcome is a variety of organizational forms that reflect the ongoing tensions and struggles that are inherent when the exploitation of creativity is the key to organizational success. In some work environments creativity may become bureaucratized and subject to tighter forms of management control than is the case in others when there are greater opportunities for autonomy, nonconformity and indeterminacy to flourish. These contrasts are discussed more fully in later chapters. In the next chapter, however, some general features of the economic role and structure of creative organizations are discussed in preparation for viewing the processes of management in a practical context.

Notes

1 There is some overlap between the concepts of post-industrial society and information society. Theories of post-industrial society emphasize the structural shift from manufacturing to services, which now accounts for more than two-thirds of all economic activity in the UK. Theories of information society stress the role of information

technology and computing and often refer to these as a dynamic source of social and intellectual creativity. For discussions of these theories see, for example, Lyon, 1986 or Webster, 1995.

2 Changes in the management disciplines concerned with behaviour in organizations reflect this. 'Industrial relations' and 'personnel management' focused on the division of labour, norms and compliance. 'Human resource management' has largely replaced them, using concepts of culture, commitment and flexibility.

2

THE CREATIVE INDUSTRIES

Creative industries include a wide variety of activities and organizations. Some, like publishing and the performing arts, have long traditions. Others, including advertising, design and mass communications, are products of the twentieth century. The most recent developments include computer software and activities taking advantage of the internet. This chapter concentrates on several creative sectors which are significant in size, economic importance and cultural significance at the present time, namely: advertising, broadcasting, music, the performing arts and publishing. In each case, there has been public debate concerning questions of management and organization. These debates, often vigorous, are explicitly concerned with the relationships between organizational and cultural creativity, public accountability, organizational efficiency and the processes of management.

Of course, the industries mentioned share many characteristics with modern organizations in general: they experience problems of growth and decline, competition, new technologies, innovation, or changing styles of work and management. In important respects, however, they are different because their 'outputs' are performances, expressive works, ideas and symbols, rather than consumer goods or services. They are at the leading edge of the movement towards the information age. It is not surprising that interest has been growing in their contribution to economic prosperity. For example, the export value of the music industry in the UK is so high (gross earnings more than trebled between 1985 and 1995, amounting to £1.2 billion) that it has become a candidate for government policy and promotion (Smith, 1998). A Creative Industries Taskforce was set up to assess the economic potential of the creative industries and seek ways to maximize it. Yet, to understand these important trends, we need to have more detailed knowledge of the organizational processes at work – especially at the point where commerce and culture meet. It is where managerial strategies are, essentially, means of organizing cultural creativity within a profit-making or efficiency-maximizing context and where creativity cannot be left to chance or individual motivation. It must be institutionalized and become part of a controlled social process.

The concept of 'creative industry' is relatively new. In popular thinking, it is more usual to refer to 'the media' as a category incorporating everything from radio and television broadcasting to newspapers, advertising, films, recorded music, the visual and performing arts. In fact, the 'media' and other creative industries are made up of very complex and different forms of organization. The concept refers to the technologies used in communication as well as the organizations that manufacture, distribute and 'transmit' cultural products. It includes the messages, symbols and ideas which are sent by them and the various ways of involving the audience in the process of reception or consumption. While there is some justification for the view that all forms of social interaction are conditioned by the media to an increasing extent – a development which Thompson describes as the 'mediazation' of contemporary culture' (1995: 46) – it does not go very far to explain how creative organizations function. Each institution, company or sector has a context and history. The purpose of this chapter is to show how the triple legacies of private commercial competition, public regulation and state subsidy affect current forms of organization in Britain, although within an increasingly competitive environment. There has been some research on creative industry organizations including the media, but very little by comparison with that undertaken in industrial manufacturing, finance or services.[1] The main evidence therefore comes from business and employment data, the regulatory framework, industry and professional bodies.

The emergence of the creative industries

The industries concerned primarily with the diffusion of information, entertainment and culture for mass consumption came into being towards the end of the nineteenth century, at about the same time as the mass production of goods for household consumption. Industrialized methods of material and cultural production played a key role in transforming lifestyles and leisure patterns. The close links between mass production, mass society and the mass media have been well documented and they show how, in the final decade of the nineteenth century, the popular press, cinema, advertising and product design began to take on a recognizably modern form. Popular publishing and popular music based on new recording technologies were soon to follow. In the early 1920s wireless broadcasting was established as a 'mass' medium and the BBC quickly attracted a nationwide audience under a unique system of public regulation and funding by licence fee. Thus, the main contours of the modern creative industries were established well before the Second World War. Privately owned companies dominated the print media – newspaper, magazine and book publishing – as well as popular recorded music, cinema and advertising. The new medium of radio was a public monopoly and there was no private competition except from foreign stations. Public broadcasting consolidated its reputation during the Second World War and the BBC, as a publicly regulated but autonomous organization, thereafter expanded its activities in both radio and the new medium of television. Alongside these was a third form of organization sustaining the performing arts: opera, theatre and orchestral music. These activities were distinguished by the role of state subsidies granted to support national artistic and cultural traditions. These three main principles of funding and organization – *private capital, indirect public support* via licence fee, and *direct state subsidy* – remain directly relevant today.

The impacts and social influence of the industries of

communication and culture during this important stage in their development were the subject of numerous investigations and theories, including the powerful but pessimistic theory of Theodor Adorno, who coined the expression 'culture industry'. He regarded the subjection of culture to industrial processes and commercial values as a profound threat to western ideals of intellectual and creative freedom (Adorno, 1991). His theory is of more than purely historical interest because it raises in a particularly sharp manner the issue of control over the creative process in organizations and culture in general. The assumption Adorno makes, writing in the 1940s, is that 'capitalism' as expressed through commercial competition is the ultimate controlling principle. The profit imperative leads to the standardization of cultural forms and to the creation of 'false needs'. This, however, was to oversimplify the issue. With the hindsight of fifty years of development in the cultural industries it is clear that capitalist production does not prescribe a single or sole solution to the problem of maximizing creativity for commercial gain, even if it is now inextricably linked with the processes of cultural production. Indeed, there are a variety of ways whereby the profit motive in the private sector is subject to the constraints of company regulation, finance, organization and control. At the same time, public accountability continues to be particularly important in the case of the BBC, the broadcasting sector in general, and the subsidized arts. The creative industries have therefore grown from different roots and they have developed with different goals and strategies. The result is a complex variety of organizational types. They are also shaped by contrasting technologies (print, sound recording, film, broadcasting, telecommunications and computing as well as traditional live performance). Technologies, in turn, are related to the scale of production, capital and unit costs, and the distribution of specialized knowledge and skills. Organizations also relate to different markets, such as those for information and entertainment; some are orientated towards production, others towards distribution (Hirsch, 1972, 1978). They respond to different needs, such as national cultural goals, elite or sectional interests, and individual consumer preferences. However, the diversity is not random and a historical perspective would suggest that there have been three main paths of development throughout the twentieth century, each weighted according to the priority of *commercial, political* or *cultural* aims.[2]

The commercial model

The first type of organization is the privately owned company, typically found in the print sector, including the newspaper, periodical and publishing industries. They have in common not only their private or public limited company status but a production system which combines the individual creative skills of the writer, journalist, photographer or designer with the coordinating skills of editors to produce a printed product capable of being mass manufactured and distributed. The newspaper, magazine or book is purchased as a commodity by individuals and becomes an object of 'private' consumption. At an early stage in their history, organizations such as newspaper corporations and publishing houses became distinctive in their ownership and entrepreneurial style. The newspaper 'barons' of the early twentieth century, such as Beaverbrook, Northcliffe and Rothermere, were powerful figures who used their businesses to exercise political and cultural influence as well as to make money – which they also did with great success. Today's equivalents are not only the press barons but the so-called media 'moguls', usually international figures, who control strategies and output in even more extensive ways across a range of media industries (Tunstall and Palmer, 1991).

The typical organizational features of the printing and publishing companies in the first half of the twentieth century were linked to their family or dynastic character and their strong commitment to political, social or cultural objectives. They were highly centralized and hierarchical and the influence of the owner was reflected throughout the organization. The sense of a political or intellectual mission which motivated many newspaper proprietors and book publishers was cultivated in their businesses, sustaining what today would be described as a strong corporate identity and culture. Companies were not widely diversified; they would expand by acquiring similar activities (for example, buying other newspaper titles) and they would rarely be involved in other products or markets. For similar reasons, firms in printing and publishing were strongly national, regional or local in character and produced for relatively homogeneous markets defined by class, education and taste. Creative roles were shaped by these factors. There was close identification between authors and editors, journalists and proprietors, either through processes of direct control (such as editorial intervention by proprietors) or through a common sense of shared purpose (a correspondence between the literary aims of author and publisher). As a consequence, in addition to professional competence, personal loyalties and friendship were integral to the creative process.

Indirect public support: the licence fee model

The second model of organization is found in public service broadcasting. While private companies manufacturing radio receivers were the impetus behind early developments in broadcasting technology, the organization of programme content and transmission was from the outset a matter of political concern and intervention by government departments and the Post Office. The British Broadcasting Corporation, established by Royal Charter in 1926, was the form of organization chosen by these authorities to express the idea of a national, monopoly service, funded by the licence fee and subject to oversight by government-appointed governors. This, however, did not imply state control on a day-to-day basis. The form of organization and regulation which emerged was the outcome of lengthy political debate which reflected the feeling of the time that certain industries were natural monopolies and they should therefore be organized as public utilities in the national interest. The first Director General of the BBC, John Reith, strongly espoused this view which complemented his vision of broadcasting as a means of general cultural improvement, capable of reaching all sections of the population. In the early years of this new medium there were, by definition, no broadcasting 'professionals' in either creative or management functions, simply because it was a new medium without organizational precedents. Instead, radio developed by combining talents from journalism, education, drama, music and light entertainment with new forms such as the wireless talk (Scannell, 1991). In doing this it created new occupations and roles including those of producer, programme editor and presenter, as well as new skills such as programme scheduling and outside broadcasting. Radio broadcasting expanded rapidly, so that by 1950, there were nearly 12 million licensed receivers. Although advertising was not permitted, the licence fee provided a stable and growing source of revenue. Radio also represented a highly significant new form of cultural organization in that it attracted a mass audience as well as the participation of the nation's cultural elite in programme making (LeMahieu, 1988). Through radio, writers as well as composers, poets, academics and intellectuals were able to address a large popular audience which was thought of as the 'listening public', and not consumers of individual products or programmes.

Broadcasting as a medium and as a form of organization therefore differs from publishing in a number of important ways. It was established at a time when the transmission technologies were limited in their capacity to use bandwidth; 'spectrum scarcity' became a powerful argument for public regulation. The means of production were not available to broadcasters except through the BBC operating as a monopoly provider and under a system of public regulation. The medium itself, using a centralized form of 'indiscriminate' transmission to the widest possible public, was limited solely by the power of transmitters. Radio, therefore, developed as an uninterrupted 'flow' of programmes. It was orientated towards the general public and was typically experienced as a family activity. The cost to the consumer was not calculated in terms of commodity prices, as with books and newspapers, but was paid for in the form of a 'tax' (the licence fee). This distancing of the commercial relationship between broadcasters and their audiences was to be an important and enduring aspect of the organizational culture of public service broadcasting – including television when it replaced radio as the dominant medium. As Burns described in his study of the BBC in the 1960s and 1970s, it resembled a state bureaucracy in its hierarchies, divisions of responsibility, and internalized sense of public duty towards the audience (1977: 45–6). It did not view itself as providing services to paying customers or satisfying consumer demand, but rather as pursuing a 'cultural' mission. Thus, Burns describes the BBC as a 'cultural bureaucracy', the features of which will be discussed later.

29

The state subsidy model

Theatres, orchestras, museums and galleries, opera and dance companies represent a third model of cultural organization. All but a limited number of the most popular and successful shows and events are commercially unpredictable and even precarious. Some live entertainment – like a rock concert – can be treated essentially as a form of advertising and marketing for recordings and other products. In the case of opera, orchestral music or dance, however, some kind of subsidy or sponsorship is essential because box office receipts or tie-ins cannot cover the costs of production. An orchestral concert or a short series of opera performances involves large numbers of people in rehearsals and preparations over weeks as well as the associated costs of facilities, publicity and promotion. The rationale surrounding subsidies and the form these take is important in shaping any organization which is dependent upon this source of finance. The Arts Council, established by Charter to develop and improve the knowledge, understanding and practice of the arts, has been the main mechanism for the distribution of state subsidies to the arts in Britain. The National Lottery now has an important supplementary role and business sponsorship plays a part as well, but on a much smaller scale. Few, if any, organizations now survive on subsidies alone and there are always strong incentives for them to operate as profit-making businesses supplying cultural products designed to appeal to as many consumers as possible.

The justification for state subsidies tends to be in terms of artistic value, innovation, preserving tradition, and the need for education, where market demand is insufficient. This creates a tension between artistic value and financial viability that is more apparent than in other creative industries. Subsidies require justification in artistic terms but they cannot avoid the language of finance. Their purpose is to compensate for a commercial 'deficit'. Although state subsidies represent a minute fraction of the total economic activity in the 'arts' sector, their importance is far greater. They are the means of survival for a diverse range of organizations which, because of subsidy support, can enjoy a considerable degree of autonomy in order to experiment and innovate without the need to have an immediate market impact. As a result, subsidies sustain occupations, careers, styles of management and organizational cultures that are quite distinct from either the cultural bureaucracy of the BBC or the profit-orientated creative industries in private ownership.

The financial structure and organization of other creative sectors may combine features from more than one of these models. The UK film industry, for example, clearly operates within the market system but it has at various times received state support by way of direct subsidy, a levy on ticket sales to raise money for production, and quotas on foreign imports. The recorded music industry is organized on a market basis in terms of record sales but it is also closely linked with broadcasting as a parallel means of distribution.

Using these models of organization, it is possible to trace the evolution of the creative industries over recent decades. It is characteristic of capitalistic forms of economic organization that they perpetually seek out new areas of investment for profit. The three models serve as a reminder that the creative industries in Britain are by no means totally absorbed into this process, certainly by comparison with the United States. The most important developments in the post-war period have been the general growth in size and importance of the sector as a whole, increasing competition, the trend towards commercialization of activities in public broadcasting and the subsidized arts, the convergence of technologies, the erosion of boundaries between hitherto separate cultural forms, and the growing international reach of markets.

Current trends

There are a number of possible indicators of growth and change in the creative industries. Figures for employment give a useful general idea of the scales of activity in different sectors although there are some difficulties in interpreting employment categories. This is because the nature of many creative occupations has changed in line with developments in technology and new forms of production. The task of an author, for example, may not be fundamentally different today compared with thirty years ago, but methods of working have been transformed through the use of computing and information technology for research, writing and delivering the final product. Data on trends show there has been a significant increase in some, but not all, categories of employment. According to one definition, in 1994 there were 560,000 people working in cultural-sector industry and occupations.[3] A more inclusive definition of cultural industries – including crafts, design, graphics, fashion, advertising and journalism – would more than double that figure to 1.5 million people in over 1000 businesses, with an annual turnover of £50 billion, contributing almost 4 per cent of GDP (Office for National Statistics, 1998). The overall growth in the numbers employed hides some significant variations which emerged strongly in a context of reregulation and liberal market reforms in the 1980s. New media technologies, firms' restructuring, and new employment practices such as incentives to self-employment and small business formation, were reflected in an increase in the numbers of cultural workers operating 'on their own account'. For example, 67 per cent of those working in the visual, literary and performing arts were self-employed and 37 per cent of those working in radio and television were either self-employed or in a temporary job. Publishing and related occupations in printing declined with trends in concentration and use of new technologies, by 5 per cent between 1987 and 1996 (Policy Studies Institute, 1999: 11). Many such changes are associated with general trends away from employment linked with manufacturing to employment in service and managerial occupations. Growth has been particularly strong in marketing, distribution, public relations and promotional activities. The changing pattern of employment in broadcasting also reflects the growth of new, often very small, companies in the independent sector as well as the tendency for the BBC (which at its peak had well over 30,000 employees, now about 20,000) and large commercial broadcasting companies to minimize permanent staff.

However, the ebb and flow in occupations and employment fails to reflect the expansion of output. Developments in technologies for data processing, printing and publishing, sound recording, and still and moving image production have contributed to large increases in productivity. These are reflected in figures for quantities of books and records published, films and videos released, newspapers sold, as well as broadcast hours.

Between 1987 and 1997, for example, the total number of new books and new editions grew by 83 per cent (Policy Studies Institute, 1999). Since the early 1980s, with the addition of Channel 4 and Channel 5 as well as cable and satellite channels, the hours of television transmission available to UK viewers have increased at an even faster rate.[4] Technical constraints on the number of channels are being removed as digital services replace the current technology. Average television viewing hours (already high by comparison with most countries at around 25 hours per week) cannot grow at the same rate and, in fact, there is some evidence that listening and viewing are in slight decline. This helps to explain the increasingly intense pressure on modern broadcasting companies to maintain their share of the audience. Film and video distribution has also seen substantial growth. After reaching a low point in 1984, cinema attendance has grown dramatically, annual admissions more than doubling to 124 million in 1994. Total advertising expenditure in the UK grew from £6.5 billion in 1987 to £13 billion in 1997 (Advertising Association, 1998). These figures provide a brief view of the supply of selected cultural products and services. All these trends are closely linked with the growth of leisure time, the increasing amounts of disposable income available to the majority of households, and the diversification of cultural output.

Concentration and integration

The general growth of cultural production and consumption has long-term significance for industrial structure, employment, leisure patterns and material culture. However, the nature of the growth and development of creative organizations raises further issues. Two concepts are of particular importance because they relate directly to issues of managerial strategy and organizational control. The first is *concentration*, which concerns the extent to which ownership, output and markets are heterogeneous or homogeneous. The second is the degree of *integration* of activities within an industry or between industries. Markets in general are rarely 'perfect' and cultural markets certainly do not involve an equal balance of players. It is apparent that creative industries display processes of concentration and monopolistic competition similar to those found in other industries. The tendency was clearly evident from an early stage in the press but by the 1950s and 1960s it had become a feature of all cultural sectors. Concentration was criticized on both economic and cultural grounds. Adorno's critique has already been mentioned. In the 1960s, 'counter-culture' was another expression of defiance against this dominant trend. Academic research on the political economy of culture industries in the 1970s found evidence that levels of ownership concentration were typically as high or even higher than in other sectors of the economy (Murdock and Golding, 1977). This fitted well with the prevailing sociological theories of capitalist ideology and the view that broadcasting and other creative industries were an extension of capitalist domination into hitherto 'autonomous' areas of culture. For example, in the newspaper, book publishing, record and film distribution sectors in the UK, Murdock and Golding found that 80 per cent of output (circulation, sales, attendance) was controlled by no more than five major companies. This seemed to provide a strong case for condemnation of the market place as an instrument to promote cultural creativity and diversity. However, this conclusion needs to be qualified. The measure of ownership concentration needs to be considered alongside other measures of concentration: that is, in *products* and in *formats* (Neumann, 1991). Product concentration refers to the proportion of output, the 'hits', which contribute to profitability. Only a minority of books, records or films are financially successful and these have to compensate for losses elsewhere. According to stock analysts quoted in Neumann, the rule of thumb is that 80 per cent of the income is derived from 20 per cent of the output (1991: 139). It is not possible to predict with any certainty which products will be successful. This unpredictability provides a stimulus to both creativity and diversity which may run counter to the apparent logic of mass, standardized production. A further indicator of concentration is the variety of formats or genres within each media sector. In the case of recorded music, for example, there are a number of formats including singles, cassettes, compact discs and music videos. However, CDs (with their standard features of length, sound reproduction, price and styles of packaging) accounted for 48 per cent of all units sold in 1994

(BPI, 1995). In terms of musical styles about 64 per cent of album sales are rock and pop. In broadcasting, especially commercial radio and satellite broadcasting, there is a tendency for a limited number of popular formats to predominate, particularly at peak audience times. Evidence from the United States suggests that despite the increase in the number of channels available, the range and diversity of programmes has declined (Dominick and Pierce, 1976; Blumler and Spicer, 1990). On the other hand, recent changes in legislation for commercial radio in the UK have encouraged diversification and allowed a new range of specialized local services to develop alongside the prevailing formats of news, talk and pop.

Thus, concentration of ownership does not automatically lead to other types of concentration. The development of new technologies and formats encourages – initially at least – innovation and diversity in forms of content. The inherent uncertainties and risks in creating and developing new products which consumers will demand are another source of stimulus to both quantity and variety. These are important elements in the dynamic of media organization which seek, on the one hand, the classic advantages of economies of scale and the largest possible market share while aiming, on the other hand, to stimulate and to keep up with volatile movements of popular taste and fashion. The strategies of media companies for integration – both vertical and/or horizontal – are a response to the business risks and organizational problems which fluctuations in public demand and fashion create. Studies of trends in ownership concentration have shown that there are fluctuations as large firms adjust their strategies or as new firms expand and become influential. In the recorded music industry, for example, Peterson and Berger (1975) show that in the USA there was a higher degree of ownership concentration between 1948 and 1959 than between 1960 and 1964. They associated this 'low' with a burst of new styles of music and the creation of a large number of new but relatively small firms. The craft nature of music production means that some aspects of the process cannot be fully industrialized (Straw, 1993). Industry concentration has increased again since that time but the example shows that it is neither irreversible nor one-dimensional (Rothenbuhler and Dimmick, 1982; Lopes, 1992). What is most striking about the large companies which currently dominate the world music industry (EMI, Polygram, Sony, Warner and Bertelsmann) is not just the degree of ownership concentration but their relationship to other activities in large international conglomerates. There are two forms of corporate expansion. The first is through a strategy of vertical integration based upon extending control over all elements of the production process from the acquisition of raw materials to processing, manufacture, marketing and distribution. The other is by horizontal integration combining businesses which are assumed to complement each other in at least some respects. An example of the first would be a newspaper publishing company which owns its printing presses and has interests in pulp and newsprint production. An example of the second would be a multimedia conglomerate with business interests in broadcasting, publishing and records, which operate separately but within an overall corporate strategy and framework of financial control. The logic of such combinations is to exploit new areas of profitability and to build complementary strengths. There was a strong move towards creating such conglomerates in the 1970s (when, for example, Thorn EMI was created out of various companies with interests in electrical goods manufacture, TV rental and recorded music). However, these trends are quite volatile. The movement of the 1980s and 1990s has been to de-merge unrelated activities, such as Thorn electrical goods from EMI music, to focus on key network links and create multinational entertainment and leisure conglomerates. The aim is to compete in the new technologies and developing markets by combining economies of scale with new possibilities for merging and developing expertise across traditional boundaries. This is particularly evident in the international links between film and television production, distribution and broadcasting.

The highly visible activities of multimedia conglomerates and household-name moguls such as Richard Branson, Michael Green, Clive Hollick and Rupert Murdoch should not be allowed to obscure an important fact about the organizational structure of the creative industries. There are limits to vertical integration arising from the uncertainties of the cultural creative process itself. Artists, writers, performers and producers are often not 'integrated' into such organizations through permanent or long-term employment. They operate on the periphery or margins, linked by agents, contracts and usually short-term association with the organizations using their services. Many are freelance, others operate in partnerships or small businesses. Their cultural significance is that they provide a seedbed for creativity, for ideas and experimentation which a larger company would have difficulty nurturing in a commercially viable way. The risks for a creative company are undoubtedly higher than in the comparable research and development activities of a manufacturing firm, where the process of innovation can be framed in terms of scientific methods and prediction. Activities such as writing, performing, composing and designing are therefore concentrated among the self-employed and small or temporary enterprises. In other sectors of the creative industries the preponderance of freelancing individuals is not so great but, even so, there is still an emphasis on the smaller scale, as in advertising and public relations. It is not surprising that the areas of the arts and media which carry the highest commercial risks – the avant-garde, experimental or minority styles, or live performances – are those least likely to be part of an integrated structure of commercial organization. They are most likely to depend on patronage or to receive public support through subsidies.

In summary, the creative industries share many features in common with business activity in general. In the UK, there is a 'mixed economy' with public broadcasting continuing to play a major role but there is virtually no aspect of creative production existing apart from market forces. There have been rapid and large-scale changes in the sector, especially since the 1980s. The circumstances which have brought these about are both exogenous (the climate of deregulation, intensified competition, European integration) and endogenous (the adoption of new information and communications technologies). However, the tensions between commerce and culture, and between creativity and control, remain. It is against this general background that the present state of the main sectors and organizational forms of the UK creative industries are examined.

Television broadcasting

Until the passing of the 1990 Broadcasting Act, UK television was a national public service in the sense that it was universally available and highly regulated by public bodies – the BBC and the Independent Broadcasting Authority.[5] It is sometimes not appreciated that, although ITV is a network of commercial companies, their business affairs and output were tightly supervised by broadcasting legislation. Under these statutes, and the BBC's Charter, television programme making was a largely national industry buttressed by steady growth in licence fee revenue for the BBC and advertising revenue for ITV. Regulation encouraged cultural bureaucracy in the BBC (Burns, 1977) and some similar features in ITV, although on a smaller scale. The public service mission had top priority and the strategies and structures of television reflected this. Public service criteria muted the competition for audiences. Employment was relatively stable. Divisions of labour were marked because production technologies were complex and unreliable, giving craft workers considerable autonomy and strength in the labour process (McKinlay and Quinn, 1999).

The 1990 Act was designed to accelerate change in the industry from this highly regulated and protected state of affairs to one of more open competition and less intervention. Today public regulation is still important but it demands less control over programme content and allows more business freedom.[6] It also enshrines the European Directives designed to promote a single market in television programmes as in other goods and services. A basis was thereby established for the UK television industry to join other industries in the international market place. Although the 1990 Act only covered commercial television (including Channels 4 and 5, cable and satellite channels), its impact was also felt by the BBC, which could not remain unaffected by these changes. It came under strong pressure to rationalize its activities on more business-orientated lines, spurred initially by the Thatcher government and by the Charter review in 1996. Rationalization across the television industry is visible in a number of ways. The BBC and the ITV companies instituted a series of budgetary reductions, curtailing the resources available for programme making. These also resulted in significant shedding of in-house staff. This process was driven by government insistence on a 25 per cent quota of independently produced programmes across the television industry based on the belief that they would be more cost-effective than in-house production. The quota was accepted – even with some enthusiasm – and a policy of Producer Choice in the BBC extended it even further into a quasi internal market for programme services. The state of affairs sometimes described as a 'comfortable duopoly', according to which the BBC and the independent sector each settled for approximately half the audience share, has been eroded by the appearance of new satellite channels and cable providers. As more television channels become available, the BBC's audience share is likely to diminish further, weakening the case for a universal licence fee. Comparable pressures within ITV are expressed through competition for advertising, leading to lower prices and a resulting impact on programme budgets. One way for a television company to reduce its central costs is to shift the emphasis from programme production to distribution – to become a 'publisher–provider'. This explains a trend in the 1990s for some ITV companies to divest themselves of major production facilities.[7]

The television industry is diverse and undergoing rapid change. There is no such thing as a typical television company. Even though the BBC remains a large national organization with a strong corporate identity and the companies in the ITV system exist within a common framework of regulation, there is a great variety of organizational forms. Alongside the BBC and the independent television companies, there is also the independent production sector. Estimates vary as to its size, but it is made up of a large number of mainly small and medium-sized businesses. A few are large but the majority consist of a single producer and, perhaps, a secretary or production assistant. As many as 400 were set up in the early 1980s in response to the opening of Channel 4, half of whose programme budget was dedicated to independent production. Some were created by ITV companies to exploit opportunities on Channel 4 and in other markets. Others were established as a result of more recent processes of rationalization in the industry. Staff made redundant in larger companies have set up their own businesses on the basis of their specialist skills which they are able to sell to other businesses in the sector (Tunstall,

1993). Many choose or are forced to operate across a number of different activities – corporate video production, TV commercial production, facilities hire and training, for example. Some, on the other hand, specialize in one type of TV programme, such as wildlife documentaries or sport, while others are established specifically to make a particular series of programmes. Each type of company represents a practical solution to the common problem of managing the creative process within an environment of cultural and commercial competition.

Radio broadcasting

Until 1973, radio in the UK was the almost exclusive preserve of the BBC. Up to that point it had developed as part of public service broadcasting rather than as a market-orientated industry. Pirate broadcasting in the 1960s brought the first taste of national competition although it was not a direct threat to revenue. Independent local radio, licensed under the 1973 Broadcasting Act, offered the first legitimate, commercially funded radio service in the United Kingdom. Like television, this was heavily regulated on public service lines similar to those influencing the BBC. The two systems – one financed from the licence fee, the other from the sale of advertising airtime – are, however, in competition for audiences. The 1990 Broadcasting Act curtailed many of the regulations on independent radio and encouraged the sector to expand. The Act's provision for the structure of the independent radio sector led to licences for national network commercial stations; low-power community stations; and the removal of restrictions on the amount of advertising time that stations could sell. However, ownership continued to be restricted to 15 per cent of potential listenership and stations became licence holders directly responsible for their own output rather than operating as franchise holders appointed by the radio authority. All these measures were designed to stimulate competition in a looser regulatory environment.

Company structures in radio reflect the history of public service at national and local levels. BBC Radio consists of five national networks: Radios 1 to 5, the so-called national regions of Northern Ireland, Scotland and Wales and the network of local radio stations, each covering a city or county. They operate within the hierarchical framework of BBC management, reporting ultimately to the Director General. Most of the BBC's radio output is produced in-house by staff producers who commission freelance contributors, for example reporters and scriptwriters. There is, however, a trend towards commissioning independent production – in keeping with government policy which requires a quarter of the BBC's total broadcast output to be independently produced. Independent radio consists of a large number of local radio stations and national networks of more recent origin, such as Classic FM. At the same time, 'incremental' stations have been licensed to reach small geographical communities or niche audiences. This feature underlines the general trend for radio to become increasingly differentiated in terms of taste, regions and the socio-demographic profile of the audience. The system has therefore expanded steadily since the first local station, Capital Radio, opened in 1973 and it now has virtually universal coverage. As independent radio has developed, a number of factors have influenced its structure. Notably, despite the appearance of fragmentation, there has been a tendency for company mergers and acquisitions to take place, enabled by a more relaxed approach by the Radio Authority. In this respect, the organization of radio – especially local radio – illustrates an interesting paradox of creative industry management. Radio is one of the most market-driven, formulaic and streamlined of all cultural products, yet it must be sensitive to local or specialized cultures to be successful. It shows very clearly how organizations must respond to the twin imperatives of commerce and culture.

Book publishing

Book publishing is a heterogeneous industry with firms of all sizes and a wide range of products aimed at both general and specialized markets. There are estimated to be between 8000 and 9000 publishing companies in the UK, ranging from very large international groups to highly specialized or sole trader publishers (Policy Studies Institute, 1998: 10). The total value of sales in 1997 was £2.8 billion. The sector is quite sharply polarized between the large conglomerates and smaller concerns. Both are an essential part of the dynamic of publishing. Five multinationals account for between one-third and one-half of the total market share. In order of size they are: Harper Collins (part of News Corporation), Random House (Bertelsmann), Reed Elsevier, Macmillan and Penguin (Pearson). There was steady annual growth in the number of new titles and editions published until 1996, when the total number was 101,504. It fell slightly in 1997 and there was speculation that this might be because firms were attempting to consolidate their efforts on the titles most likely to be profitable or because the market is beginning to move away from print-based media. Behind these figures lies a story of major reconstruction in the industry, in response to developments in technology, economic cycles, internationalization, as well as a continuous increase in consumer spending. This includes spending on book purchases which, with newspapers and other publications, are on average the fourth largest item of leisure expenditure in UK households (Central Statistical Office, 1995).

A wave of mergers and acquisitions in the 1980s produced a group of internationally based companies which, by the mid-1980s, controlled over half the domestic market (Clark, 1988; Feather, 1993). They adopted strategies for improving efficiency and minimizing overheads, for example by amalgamating the marketing sections of previously separate divisions or companies. Financial criteria became more explicit in publishing decisions and management processes became more profit-orientated. Most large companies made significant numbers of employees redundant. Among the large companies is Harper Collins, which became part of Rupert Murdoch's News Corporation as a result of two acquisitions in 1987 and 1989. Penguin/Longman is the largest UK-owned publisher and part of the Pearson Group, a media conglomerate with interests in regional newspapers, the *Financial Times*, satellite broadcasting and information technology. The history of this group illustrates the transformation that has occurred in the publishing industry. Both Longman and Penguin were long-established companies, founded in 1724 and in the 1920s respectively. Penguin had virtually created the UK paperback market which flourished from the 1930s and which grew massively in the 1960s. It encountered problems in the 1970s, partly because of its excessively lengthy title list. Peter Mayer, its

American-born chairman, led the corporate turnaround. Other companies, including Michael Joseph and Hamish Hamilton, acquired in the 1980s, were regrouped into a number of organizational divisions after 1988. Similarly Reed, the second largest UK book publisher, has undergone a number of fundamental changes. Its book interests were established as part of an earlier conglomerate strategy around 1970, beginning with Hamlyn Books. Hamlyn was later sold back to its original owner and later (in 1987) reacquired, by which time it had itself become a small empire (Octopus/Hamlyn/Mitchell Beazley). In the space of about 40 years, Reed had moved from its original base in paper and newsprint manufacture, through a period of diversification, to a more focused group emphasis on book publishing. The next phase of this complicated journey was the merger in 1993 with the Dutch group Elsevier to create a European multinational business to compete with the largest global corporations in the publishing field such as Bertelsmann and News Corporation.

The relatively low costs of entry into publishing allow for the constant replenishment of small firms (Hirsch, 1985). Some are an outlet for specialists and enthusiasts but the new small publishing firm may also be an avenue for highly experienced and talented staff who have made a career in major publishing houses. Their motive may be to redirect their efforts, rekindle direct relationships with authors, or fulfil a literary ambition. Many of these businesses are started by those who have been made redundant through the rationalization of the industry. However, alongside this there has been significant restructuring of employment, not simply the shedding of staff. A study of careers in UK book publishing showed that there were substantial numbers of self-employed editors and proof readers who had spent part of their career as employees in publishing houses but now work freelance (Granger *et al.*, 1995). However, the largest single group in their sample was the 'refugees' who had experienced involuntary redundancy. One of the positive attractions of working freelance is that it allows more control over when, what and how work is to be done. This element of control is likely to have an increasing appeal when financial and marketing priorities take precedence over the literary and creative aspects. Book publishing provides many illustrations of the changing dynamics of media industry as companies seek out the forms of organization which are most likely to combine efficiency and flexibility without losing contact with the vital sources of creative energy and 'product innovation'.

Recorded music

The music industry in Britain employs over 115,000 people, either directly or in closely related or dependent services and industries. According to one of the most comprehensive studies of the UK record industry, the six largest firms account for 70 per cent of popular music recordings (Negus, 1992). But the impression of high economic concentration which this gives needs to be qualified, as Negus points out, by looking at the complex relationships between the large, conglomerate firms and the 'labels' they own or influence. It is not a tight, hierarchical relationship of control over musical ideas or content (even if there are mechanisms for strict financial control) but a somewhat flexible, self-correcting relationship between the parent and smaller units which are more sensitive and responsive to market changes (Hennion, 1983; Negus 1995, 1998; Hesmondhalgh, 1996). Pop and disco recordings, which are the largest part of the business, account for nearly two-thirds of the market. The combined market share of the second range of record companies is about 20 per cent and they are typically geared towards particular styles, including rock, reggae, jazz, country and folk. The substratum of the industry, which has over 1000 companies, involves an even wider range of production labels as well as studios, promoters, booking agencies, venues and artists' management. The typical problem for managers of record and music publishing companies is that only a small proportion of their output can be expected to make a profit. For example, only one in ten of new pop releases are profitable. Therefore, companies have to balance their successes with new and untested material that will generate opportunities for future success. Larger companies can 'insure' themselves for success by using well-tried formulae with good marketing and promotion. This allows them to achieve a success rate for new singles releases of four or five out of ten recordings entering the top 40. They can also buy a stake in smaller companies which have already absorbed the risks of developing new styles and untried artists. The small producers are not therefore victims of an oligopoly but active and flexible components in a multifaceted industry. Organizational creativity is not the exclusive preserve of one type of production.

The growth in the domestic as well as the export market for recorded music allowed the larger companies to expand and diversify during the 1980s and 1990s. This was a rather different strategy of diversification from the formation of conglomerates in the 1970s, when it was not unusual for companies to expand sideways into unrelated or very distantly related activities. Traditionally, there were ties between record companies and electronics manufacturers – such as Phillips – and some of the diversification can be explained by the companies' strategy of keeping control of rapidly changing technologies and formats. But there were examples of diversification into electrical goods (Thorn EMI), lighting and defence (Phillips), as well as airlines (Virgin). In most cases these trends have been reversed. The new element in the recent period is the liberalization of the ownership regime in television and radio, and the convergence between music in film, video and computer software as well as sound recording. This allows the record companies to pursue strategies of diversification which have more 'synergy' with their interest in music and which offer ways to control the growing competition from broadcasting, film and video. Thus Time Warner, Bertelsmann, Sony, EMI and other international, multimedia entertainment companies have positioned themselves to exploit creative output and the rights to its reproduction in any format or location. One of the consequences for management is that the core activity of producing records is refocused on rights and the branding of artists across a range of creative industries.

Advertising

The number of people employed in the member agencies of the Institute of Practitioners of Advertising in 1999 was 12,750. However, the Creative Industries Taskforce calculates that all companies whose business depends on advertising employ a total of 4.5 million people. This is consistent with the growing commercial importance of branding and the shift in the modern service economy towards demand creation rather than supply management. Fluctuations in employment often illustrate quite dramatically the vulnerability of advertising to short-term changes in the economic climate. The industry tended to thrive in the aggressively entrepreneurial atmosphere of the 1980s. However, in the early 1990s it suffered a significant downturn from which it has now recovered. This is not the only source of fluctuations. The advertising industry is notoriously fissiparous, partly because of its susceptibility to changes in advertising budgets and the clients' fashions. But it also sees itself as an industry that requires a regular turnover of personnel and new partnerships in order to renew the creative process. In this respect, it represents a type of creative organization which makes a virtue out of teamwork, networks and project management. The very term 'agency' used to describe advertising firms highlights this. The agency culture is both strongly commercial and highly personalized.

In the 1950s, 90 per cent of advertising expenditure in the news media was devoted to press advertising. The emphasis has steadily shifted towards television and other visual media, and towards more complex marketing and promotional packages. Systematic data on audience attitudes and behaviour are used to support commercial decisions. In fact, the amount of detailed market research that precedes any new product launch or advertising campaign tends to undermine advertising's claim to be highly flexible and creative. This has encouraged a division of labour to emerge between 'creative' and 'media' agencies. The former specialize in the process of generating ideas and developing campaigns while the latter focus on the most technically efficient ways to research, market and distribute advertising to media clients. But like other sectors of the creative industries, advertising must constantly search for ways to reduce the uncertainties and risks involved in working with the raw materials of popular taste and fashion.

The phenomenon of ownership concentration is found in advertising agencies as well as the other creative sectors (Leiss *et al.*, 1986; Mattelart, 1991). The largest firms are multinational and they account for the majority of the advertising spend by large corporate clients. The 1980s was a decade of international expansion by British firms, with significant acquisitions in America by WPP and the Saatchi brothers. The rate of mergers and acquisitions in advertising is second only to that in publishing (Pilati, 1993: 224).

However, these 'megagroups' have had a chequered history, partly due to the strategy of over-borrowing to finance expansion and partly because of deteriorating economic conditions. It is also likely that organizational problems played a part: the greater the spread, the more difficult it is to maintain personal networks, client trust, confidentiality and creative partnerships. Size is not the only factor in attracting large and profitable accounts; in creative agencies, reputation counts above all else. A small but successful creative partnership may be sufficient to attract a large account, and this offers a regular incentive to the formation of new partnerships and agencies. However, with the growth in scale and competitiveness, the overall emphasis in advertising has shifted from the cultural, 'creative' aspects to commercial aspects.

The performing arts

The performing arts (including theatre, opera, dance and live music) are small in scale when compared with the other sectors and they are fragmented in their organization. Theatre, for example, involves some 350 companies working at 600 venues. Finance for production comes from a combination of box office takings, local authority or central government subsidy channelled through the Arts Council and other agencies, sponsorship and other earnings (Myerscough, 1988). The proportion of subsidy has not remained constant. In the 1960s and 1970s, subsidies were increased when commercial theatres were threatened with closure because of rising costs and declining audiences. Outside London, local authorities increasingly took on the role of supporting arts at the local and regional level. During the 1980s, however, the real value of subsidies was eroded and policies were aimed at improving marketing and management so that levels of public subsidy could be reduced. Commercial theatre audiences (essentially in London's West End) maintained their levels throughout the decade. A more commercial ethos now pervades the subsidized theatre although some level of public support will continue to be used as a means to promote new talent, provide training, encourage diversity of output and access for sections of the population who would otherwise be denied. With no prospect of an increase in subsidy, performing arts companies have had to explore other avenues, which include cutting staff, reducing the number or complexity of performances, curtailing touring plans, or even closure (Policy Studies Institute, 1995; Sierz, 1997).

The issue of public subsidy and its relationship to commercial forms of management is dramatically illustrated by the case of the Royal Opera House, Covent Garden, which in 1986 received 56 per cent of its revenue from central government sources (Policy Studies Institute, 1986). By 1992 the figure had fallen to 38 per cent. The crisis continued and a major report in 1998 recommended an increase in the subsidy in line with practice in most other European countries. The debate is instructive not least because it has been conducted in a very detailed and public way, and because its main exchanges reveal the conflicting artistic and economic responses to a seemingly endless debt crisis. The aesthetic arguments are the same as they have always been: a national centre for opera should aspire to the highest possible artistic standards and if the costs cannot be met from ticket sales alone, they must be subsidized as necessary. This argument is strengthened by the assertion that access to the treasures of opera (like other priceless assets in the arts) should not be denied to those who cannot afford the real cost. On the other hand, there are the arguments for consumer sovereignty, for minimizing the burden on the public purse, and for precise measurement of costs and benefits. It is unlikely that there will ever be a neat or satisfactory solution to these dilemmas. The debate, however, revolves in practice around the question of whether the creative process can actually be 'managed' or placed under a rigid financial discipline and what styles of management are appropriate in such a context.[8] The rapid turnover of managerial personnel suggests that the answer still has to be found. Some may see it as a sign of progress that the term 'arts management' has begun to replace the older term 'arts administration', which located the process of control in the tradition of enlightened public authorities and supervision by devoted amateurs.

Conclusion

In this chapter, we have identified the main features and trends in the *commercial, publicly regulated* and *state subsidized* sectors of the creative industries. The examples illustrate that the principles on which they are based are distinctly different. In practice, of course, their boundaries are inevitably more blurred and there are overlaps between one sector and another. The reasons for this include the processes of horizontal and vertical integration which have been described, as well as the opportunities for convergence opened up by developments in information and communications technologies. Furthermore, business fashions and the idiosyncrasies of owners and chief executives account for variations from the 'standard' patterns. Cross-ownership and cross-promotion between sectors have become more common, as, for example, in the relationships between film, television and publishing. Collaboration increasingly involves otherwise unrelated sectors of activity, such as when financial services support concert or opera performances, and when drinks brands sponsor football clubs. Within many organizations which are not involved in 'creative' products or services as such, the functions of advertising, marketing and public relations play an increasingly important role. For all these reasons, the management of creativity is relevant to an increasingly wide range of organizations.

The changes that have occurred in the creative organizations in recent years have brought problems of management and organization into the foreground of public debate. At the same time, they have produced a variety of practical responses or solutions to the endemic problem of reconciling innovation, cultural aims and the uncertainties of the creative process with financial and managerial priorities. At a later stage in the book we will present the main alternatives in the form of a typology which builds on and elaborates the themes of this chapter, namely the distinctive forms of management associated with the commercial, public service and subsidized sectors and their responses to recent trends. The next chapter, however, presents a more detailed analysis and discussion of what we mean by the 'creative process' and how it relates to theories of management and organization.

Notes

1 Some significant contributions to the study of broadcasting organizations and production include Burns (1977), Daymon (1997) and Elliott (1972, 1977).

2 Miège uses a political economy classification which has some similarities to this. However, his 'commodity', 'flow' and 'information' types of communication media owe more to differences in the technologies of delivery than the categories in the present account (see Miège *et al*. 1986; Miège, 1987, 1989).

3 Policy Studies Institute (1996). The categories were based on the UK Labour Force Survey and included publishing, recording, films, radio and television, literary and performing arts, museums, libraries and archives. The number also includes managers, archivists and artists working in cultural occupations in other industries.

4 In a typical week, terrestrial television hours alone grew from 471 in 1985 to 671 in 1995 (Policy Studies Institute, 1996: 85).

5 The 1990 Broadcasting Act replaced the IBA with the Independent Television Commission, which licenses and regulates terrestrial, cable and satellite television.

6 Some have announced the demise of public service broadcasting (e.g. Tracey, 1998) but this is premature. Even in countries such as Italy where broadcasting culture is strongly commercial, the public element remains strong. Of course, it has had to adapt to competition.

7 For example Meridian, the new ITV company which replaced Southern Television in 1993. However, as Daymon shows, there were some signs of a reversal in this new trend after a few years (1997). For a discussion of the limits to flexible specialization in the television sector, see Saundry (1998) and Saundry and Nolan (1998).

8 See, for example, the two 1992 reports: one internal report commissioned from Price Waterhouse and an external report from the Arts Council.

3

THE ORGANIZATION OF CREATIVE WORK

In this chapter, we consider how a range of organizations typically structure their work activities to protect, encourage and enhance their creativity and to what extent they still resort to formalized bureaucratic operating procedures in their attempts to overcome the inherent uncertainties of cultural work. The evidence is from two main sources (for a more detailed description, see the Appendix on research methods). First, there is the documentary evidence found in job descriptions, organization charts, occupational statistics, training manuals and career guidance literature. Many organizations can provide some form of job description and an organization chart but they often exist as formal statements that have little direct relevance to actual operating practices or the attainment of organizational goals. They cannot be taken at face value. In other organizations – especially small companies – 'job descriptions' simply do not exist because the division of labour and conduct of work tasks are based on informal procedures, personal negotiation and team working. In these circumstances, the organization operates as a constellation of projects and processes with loosely defined and continually fluctuating parameters. However, there is value in analysing both informal and formal ways of organizing tasks and responsibilities. They help to highlight the ambiguities of the work process within creative organizations and the attempts to solve the paradox of control and creativity. It is a paradox because the problem of reconciling openness, intuition, personal networks and individual autonomy (which serve 'creative' ends) with instrumental criteria and rational business methods can never be completely resolved.

The second type of evidence is the data elicited by interviews and observations of working practices in a range of different organizations. This provides a more nuanced description of work in particular settings and interpretations from a more personal point of view. The design of work embodies strategies for developing personal and professional identity as well as expressing an organizational purpose. The two types of data help to build up a general description of the typical structure of media occupations and the divisions of labour which are most commonly found. This in turn is a basis for analysing how general expectations of occupational roles and responsibilities are translated into practice in a variety of settings. More precisely, do they represent satisfactory 'solutions' to the tensions implicit in creative work in organizations?

Divisions of labour

Creative organizations involve complex divisions of labour designed to carry out certain essential functions. In large organizations they will normally be evident in a formal division of roles and responsibilities. In a small organization they will overlap or combine in the work of an individual or a small group. However, even where there is no clear demarcation of roles, it is possible to distinguish three conceptually distinct organizational 'functions' or activities: *production, creativity,* and *control and coordination.*

Since the *raison d'être* of a creative organization is to produce a particular form of cultural output for an audience or market, one key set of activities is directly concerned with *production.* This includes the execution of the productive tasks such as operating a camera or sound recording equipment, editing film and video, using computer software to create an image, or copy editing a text. The tasks usually involve well-defined skills and technical competences acquired through formal vocational training as well as experience. They may be quite repetitious. Performance can be graded and measured according to criteria of technical competence and output can be quantified. Tasks are defined by the technologies employed ('software' as well as 'hardware') with an occupational division of labour which has evolved in line with the development and application of new technology. Thus, for example, the work of graphic design has acquired a new dimension of skill because computers are now used to generate or manipulate texts and images. Fundamentally, the production of culture at this level involves 'craft' skills which have a recognizable technical base and rules of procedure and a distinct occupational character. In the past, and to some extent today, their identity has been expressed through occupational associations and trade unions (for example, Association of Cinematograph, Television and Allied Technicians, Broadcasting Entertainment, Cinematograph and Theatre Union, Equity or the Musicians Union). There are variations in how far production and the execution of technical tasks are incorporated into any particular company. Publishing and printing, for example, were once typically found together as parts of a single organization, but rarely so today. Television production was once invariably done 'in-house' because of cumbersome and delicate technology but today programme making, post-production activities and programme publishing are often organized separately and flexibly. The different arrangements have advantages and disadvantages which will be the subject of later discussion but for every type of cultural output there is a set of activities which involves direct use of production technologies and a 'craft' form of job design.

By its nature, modern cultural production is an interpretative activity with a premium on the ability to communicate ideas and emotions in a constantly shifting environment which can never be fully routinized. The second key element in the division of labour in creative organizations therefore concerns the *creative* function. This use of the term 'creative' is related to specific tasks within the division of labour and it reflects common usage within the creative industries. The organization of creativity, the main subject of this book, refers to the relationship between the parts of an organization. The creative function is represented by the roles and occupations which are centrally concerned with the indeterminate processes of creation which conceptualize, interpret, communicate and motivate production. At the heart of such activities (such as editing, producing and directing) are reflective, interactive and intuitive processes with an indeterminate outcome. Training for these jobs is unlikely to be delivered in vocational form as a specific set of skills. Instead, qualification comes through a high level of general education combined with learning through practice in a specific setting. This is most appropriate to tasks which involve relatively abstract systems of value such as aesthetics. Performance criteria are linked to evaluation by peers, critics and audiences rather than to purely quantitative indicators. Ambiguity and uncertainty about job titles and descriptions is greatest in this group of occupations and the social organization of work tasks is implicit rather than explicit. In a modern, profit-orientated economy the creatives who make up this group of occupations are the key agents or 'cultural intermediaries' (Bourdieu, 1993: 133–4; Bovone, 1994). They are cultural entrepreneurs, whose main trading assets are cultural knowledge, ideas, symbolic forms and interpretation. However, these are not fixed quantities but a function of relations between participants in the field of cultural production. To turn these assets into cultural forms successfully requires skilful organization to cultivate talent, stimulate individual effort and combine complementary contributions for the realization of a project.

The tasks of *coordination and control* of creative organizations are the responsibility of managers and administrators. These tasks are conceptually different from those of 'creation,' although in small organizations they are likely to be combined. They are defined according to the general aims of the organization. In the case of a commercial organization this is to compete successfully and to make a return for shareholders. A public or publicly subsidized organization may have the aim of reaching a certain kind of audience or maintaining a certain level of service or type of output. In either case, the method is to use rational means and standard procedures to achieve predetermined goals such as levels of revenue, profit, production quotas, market share, audience ratings or range of services. Performance can be measured against these aims and defended in terms of rationalistic criteria. From an occupational viewpoint, management is complex because in large organizations it is subdivided into specialisms (such as finance, personnel, sales and marketing or production management). In small organizations a wide range of activities will be carried out by a small number of managers or even a particular individual.

These three types of organizational function – *control and coordination*, the *creative* function and *production* – do not in themselves represent or describe a division of labour. Rather, they indicate a distribution of activities which are essential to the creative industries but which may not always be found elsewhere. For example, the research and development activities of a research-oriented engineering firm resemble the creative activities of a cultural organization and they pose similar problems for the management of innovation. In contrast, the creative element in a large bureaucracy, such as a bank or insurance company, is likely to be minimal. What makes creative organizations distinctive is the interface between the creative and managerial functions and the variety of ways in which this is experienced in practice. It may be the site of a sharp conflict between 'commerce' and 'culture'; it may be a place of organizational as well as individual and artistic creativity; or, most typically, a process of negotiation, mutual adjustment and compromise. These experiences are reflected in the data derived from interviews, and they are used here to categorize the forms of organization which are to be found across a range of creative industries. Observation of the fluid and shifting boundaries reveals a number of common features as well as important differences.

Television broadcasting

Television broadcasting has undergone some of the most fundamental of the changes experienced by the various media sectors as a result of the combined effects of new technology, new forms of competition and a revised system of regulation. Widespread restructuring has affected the internal dynamics of broadcasting organizations including job design. To understand the impact of this restructuring it is necessary to appreciate the organizational characteristics of the traditional public service organization as it developed in the 1960s and 1970s before the restructuring of the 1980s and 1990s. The fullest account is in the research on the BBC published by Burns (1977). His term *cultural bureaucracy* captures very well the central organizational theme, which is that, as a large-scale corporation designed and regulated to operate as a public 'utility', its form was essentially bureaucratic. Strong hierarchy, elaborate divisional structure, clear demarcation of roles and responsibilities were all present. At the same time, the BBC existed to serve a national cultural purpose and this gave the bureaucracy a distinctive 'cultural' character and discipline, which was expressed in the ideas of autonomy and professionalization among its creative cadre. Essentially, as one of Burns's respondents remarks, the role of the organization was to provide a financially secure base, creative freedom and a protected environment in which its creative workers could operate, in return for a strong commitment and close identification with the organization:

> We do have in the BBC a deep suspicion of so-called pure administration. It's a dirty word. I think personally that this is very healthy. After all, the BBC exists to put out programmes and the people putting out programmes are in the front line and all that sort of thing, and they have to have more consideration than anybody else. The rest of the chaps are there to help them in one way or another.
>
> (cited in Burns, 1977: 252)

This respondent, a senior administrator, was speaking in 1963, which helps to account for the paternalistic tone and language. Certain of these features are still recognizable, particularly in the degree of autonomy which programme makers have in the day-to-day performance of their tasks. An assistant floor manager, for example, has difficulty describing production activities in terms that conventional management theories would recognize:

> I find it very difficult to define. But when we're actually on the production it's a lot more to do with the realities and the technicalities and the problems we face rather than management. Everybody does I suppose tend to manage their own parts.

However, there have been radical changes (including those already mentioned in Chapter 1) affecting the work and relative autonomy of creative staff. The structure of the television broad-casting industry as a whole has become far more complex and diversified and this is reflected in the greater variety of types of organization.

The organization of drama production is a good illustration of the changes which have been occurring. A television drama pro-duction, whether studio-based or filmed on location, involves programme production staff including the director, scriptwriter, designer, production manager, assistant and secretary, camera, lighting and sound operators, floor/studio manager and assist-ants, engineering and other back-up services. The key role is that of the producer, who takes charge of a project from conception to completion. The actual content of a producer's job depends on the type of production. This may involve film or video, a particular genre, studio or location shooting, each of which has a particular set of artistic standards and organizational expectations already built in to the role. But typically, it includes liaison with managers and sources of finance, reading and evaluating scripts, selecting key production staff and organizing the team, making creative decisions during the production stage, supervising post-produc-tion work, and negotiating distribution. In the past, producers at the BBC were usually recruited through internal competition by staff with relevant experience. There was, and is, no clear career or promotion ladder for producers because their role is defined more by the character of the project they are working on than by their position within an organizational hierarchy. The senior producer is likely to be a highly independent and entrepreneurial indi-vidual (in the sense of cultural entrepreneurship) enjoying the prestige which is associated with responsibility for a large pro-duction team and widely recognized programmes. The role of the producer as a project manager and creative team leader has not changed substantially in recent years but the relationship be-tween producers and management in the BBC (as well as other large broadcasting organizations) has been through a sea change. The protected space within the cultural bureaucracy – where the model of the autonomous professional worker prevailed – has almost ceased to exist. There have been two main consequences. On the one hand, some producers have become subject to closer monitoring and control as employees or contractors to the organization. The large majority of producers are contracted for a specific project or series, although they still work within the setting of the larger organization, alongside management and production staff who are employees. On the other hand, some producers have chosen to distance themselves from the organization and create more space for manoeuvre by establishing independent companies. In his study of television producers, Tunstall (1993) shows that one result of this trend is for the administrative and commercial (or management) functions to become part of the independent producers' role. Thus, one of the aims of independence, that is, to widen the range of choice of programmes and projects and to give more freedom in programme production, is only partly met. Indeed, 'many independents are unsure whether to describe themselves as business executives and managers or as TV producers and programme-makers' (1993: 165). The producers collaborating in the interview survey made similar comments about their role and changes in their patterns of work. There is, first, a perception, especially among producers who have wide experience of the 'independent' or 'commercial' world, that the BBC still has some way to go to become like its competitors. The cultural bureaucracy is not seen as enabling but more as a burden. A BBC drama series manager comments that

> The problem that we have here is that the Corporation is going to go into a pseudo commercial world. We're trying to run like the outside world but actually what we do is have a lot of the constraints of a bureaucracy.

A drama producer uses similar language to convey the sense of burden:

> I think the BBC is far too top-heavy. The middle management – where that ends and begins is my role as producer. I see myself on the top of a pyramid. Above, there's an inverted pyramid, and there's a hell of a lot of people in that inverted pyramid squashing the programme makers.

Second, however, the move from staff employment to short-term contracts is seen as an essential part of the 'tightening-up' process. For example, the same producer who condemned bureaucratic constraints uses an argument for closer supervision and control in the management of producers:

> Producers who were here on staff and were not productive or didn't come up with any ideas could be sitting around doing nothing and it seemed reasonable to bring people in on a contract basis for a show – contract them at the start of the show and the end of the show – this is to do with the whole way the organization is being run. In the past run-ups were enormous and run-downs were enormous, post-production.

Another, freelance, producer contrasted the lead-in time for a short series at the BBC – which included time for the development of the script – with typical American practice, where the producer is faced with a complete script from day one. These observations show that judgements about organizational rationality tend to be myopic. Devolved organizational responsibility brings the need for 'reasonable' measures to control and coordinate activities. However, changing the boundaries of responsibility has challenged the autonomy of creative occupations in television drama without offering an alternative organizational solution except outside the dominant organizational framework.

Restructuring has led to complex changes in the organization of production. The most important shift has been from 'in-house', vertically integrated forms of programme production to 'network' processes. These not only encourage the formation of small, specialist independent companies but also a high proportion of freelance workers contracted for short periods to work on specific projects within the larger organizations. Changes in technology are associated with changes in the skill structure, including some 'deskilling' of craft work. At the same time the demand for organizational flexibility in response to cost pressures has increased the amount of 'multi-tasking' among production employees in television. Those who have traditionally undertaken specialist roles within the more technical aspects of programme making are now compelled to exercise a wider range of skills within the context of more ambiguously defined work roles, duties and responsibilities (Daymon, 1997). The IMS *Skill Search* report (Varlaam *et al.*, 1990) noted that with the rapid changes in the television, film and video industry there are no industry-wide standards of competence, even at minimum levels, relating to the various grades. And in a context where anyone in the industry can claim to be whatever he or she wishes, the traditional process by which careers are developed is to rely on 'personal networks of known talent' (p. 69). Access for freelancers is 'largely ad hoc, via "foot in the door" mechanisms' (p. 61). These features are not simply a reflection of the rapid change and disorganization of the industry, although this is an important factor. They also point to the intrinsic problems of organizing the creative work process and the unique demands of each programme-making project. In these circumstances the complete routinization of tasks is neither possible nor desirable.

Radio broadcasting

Radio broadcasting, although it is often closely linked organizationally and financially with television, has moved in a different direction. In fact, in the context of independent local radio in particular, there has been a shift towards greater role specification and tighter delineation of work tasks. In many ways 'creativity' has become routinized and organized according to various managerially imposed, standardized procedures. One reason for this is that, compared with television, radio is relatively less complex. Operations are on a smaller scale, the technology involves sound only, and output is often concerned only with a single genre of content. Technological improvements in sound recording and studio control systems have contributed to a significant amount of deskilling; in some cases to the point where a radio station may be automated to such an extent that it can broadcast without human intervention for many hours at a time. In commercial radio stations, programmes are structured on the basis of 'formats' which stipulate the selection of recorded music, its organization into playlists as well as the frequency with which presenters are instructed to mention station identity, the names of localities, and other factors closely geared to detailed research into audience profiles. Information technology allows commercials and recordings to be monitored and this data to be compared with the profile of listeners at the relevant time of day. For example, Broadcast Data Systems monitors 50 radio and music stations in Britain in this way (McCourt and Rothenbuhler, 1997: 204). Advertising is then delivered on the basis of this well-defined, highly routinized cultural product. In such a context, there is virtually no capacity for either employee creativity or programme innovation. Similarly, chart data is a commodity which is used by the industry to increase control. This may be at the expense of diversity, since the charts ignore both new and secondary markets.

There is no direct working relationship between musicians and presenters who play their music. The 'creative' focus has shifted from production to public relations, promotion and marketing, and the preparation of the appropriate software that dictates the music and voice package of programme content. An ILR sales manager outlines the changed role of the presenter in this radio version of the tension between commercial and cultural values:

> *Sales Manager:* Presenters . . . cannot do their job if you mock their ego. They have to have massive egos. You have to manage that as best you can. They have to think in that way. It's the entertainment industry on one side, and on the other side is the sales aspect. Now if the two start getting confused then that can have a phenomenal effect on your business.
>
> *Interviewer:* But, you know, I look around and I see computer software which will do most of your music selection for you. I see people producing their own shows effectively. A lot of the mystique, it seems to me, goes . . .
>
> *Sales Manager:* It has to be created deliberately in that our listeners out there have to think that our radio is fantastic. They have to think that. If they don't think that, it becomes boring and mundane, and it's likely that this radio station won't be in existence . . . So we have to create that excitement about it, so it's necessarily there. It's a question of how it's managed. It must be allowed to flourish. It must be promoted as far as the listener is concerned yet we don't want any of the negatives in terms of running the business.

In other words, the persona of the presenter is the property and symbol of the organization and controlled by the marketing strategy. The output of a popular music station, or indeed Classic FM, requires highly standardized selection, processing and presentation of a well-ordered flow of music, news, continuity and commercials. It must be strictly tailored to the audience. As an ILR managing director said: 'It's the research at the end of the day that you live or die by.' The greatest creativity lies in the identification of a cultural trend, an untapped market, and in creating the format to satisfy this unmet demand. The occupational division of labour is therefore quite simple and it offers only limited scope for career advancement. Accordingly, personal development is by moving from one radio station to the next – a movement which has been made easier because of concentration in the ownership of once separately operated companies.

Book publishing

In the world of book publishing, the central 'creative' relationship is usually understood to be that between the author and editor. With the shift away from family-owned publishing houses towards larger and more bureaucratic publishing corporations as described in Chapter 1, this relationship no longer has such a personal character. However, publishing occupations, skills and division of labour still have the same general composition. The functions of control and coordination, creative direction and production can be represented as three conceptually distinct areas of activity, not unlike those found in television. The production tasks, many of them fairly routine and repetitive, are carried out by editorial assistants, copy editors, proof readers, indexers, designers and picture researchers. A book jacket designer in a large publishing company describes the experience:

> I think in publishing you can only be so creative; there are so many restrictions and limitations as to what you can do ... You sort of pick [them] up along the way and know that certain things just won't be acceptable. And I don't think whether you're working in a large company or whether you're working as a freelance designer makes much difference. I think that sort of restriction is still there.

These occupations involve mainly autonomous and skilled forms of work undertaken without close supervision, where the parameters of the job are defined by the production schedule and a specific set of skills. It is not unusual for these to be carried out by freelance workers based at home (Baines, 1999). In some forms of publishing authors themselves have to take responsibility for some of these activities. However, production work in publishing, wherever it takes place, can in principle be made subject to measurement criteria and performance indicators typical of bureaucratic organizations. As competition between firms becomes more intense, it is a prime target for increased rationalization and intensification of work.

The role of the commissioning editor in publishing is similar to that of the producer in television. The editor is responsible for selecting authors and buying new manuscripts in accordance with the publisher's priorities and policy. Indeed, from the author's point of view, the editor is synonymous with the 'publisher'. Editorship involves detailed knowledge of relevant cultural issues and trends, strong personal networks and persuasive skills. These are needed in order to retain and encourage key authors, and the willingness to make subjective and sometimes risk-laden judgements about aesthetic value, public taste and artistic merit. Alongside these cultural tasks, the commissioning editor is responsible for project management; keeping books on schedule; agreeing contracts; liaising with literary agents, lawyers and designers; and, of course, planning and monitoring the finance for each project. The roles of manager and 'creative' are therefore combined as the editor acts both for the organization with the aim to produce a reliable return on investment and as a cultural interpreter and intermediary on behalf of the authors. This combined role is not part of a well-defined career structure. Sometimes the role may involve very little editing – a source of complaint from one literary agent:

> Publishing houses have so little time to edit these days because of the low profit margins they're facing ... Sometimes the first people to go in a recession are the editors, they're the first level of redundancies. Because of the fact that there's so little training in publishing, that editors have less and less skills, we sometimes feel that if we don't edit here, the book will be put straight into production and that's the end of it.

The typical path is upwards through the positions of copy editor and desk editor and it may eventually lead to a senior managerial position. But the most common career pattern is one of moves from one firm to another in search of higher level work; for example, more prestigious authors, larger scale projects. The inherent tension in the editor's role is well illustrated by the moves of some key editorial staff in the course of the publishing industry's recent restructuring. While mergers and takeovers have made for larger, more bureaucratic organizations, the counter-tendency for the creation of new, small publishing houses has been driven by entrepreneurial editors who wish to remain in close touch with their authors and markets. The problem is illustrated by the comments of a senior editor in a large publisher:

> What is frustrating is when I've got another layer of management over me who are making decision about books which they don't really know. I mean, it's me who has taken them on and nursed them and developed the book. And then they have the ultimate say-so about whether we can contract to publish it.

The solution of taking more direct personal responsibility for both management and editorial involves complex skills. Another editor, now managing director of a small independent literary publisher describes his motives:

> I think that the editorial aspect of publishing is the most important. It's not the only one, of course; there's marketing, production, and all the other aspects of publishing, but if you don't have books and authors you can't actually start publishing at all. I found that my own editorial basis was being eroded and one of the reasons for this, in a big corporation, I think, was that inevitably if one big corporate company buys a series of smaller companies, it wants to integrate them.

Referring to his own small company formed after he left an expanding conglomerate, this editor identified the sources of satisfaction in an independent operation which come from closer contact with authors as well as involvement in a combined spectrum of strategic, administrative and creative activities:

The smaller the company, the more the overall interest becomes but, you know, we have exactly the same bits and pieces that any publishing company would have. There is a finance director, there is a production director, there is a sales director, there is a publicity director . . . You need a sort of creative streak, because you need to see a book and an author and you need to try and plan how that book can be improved. You need marketing skill. Most publishers should take an overall view of the book; in other words, they should have a concept of what it is going to look like, and so on. And attention to details is important and diplomacy is important if you are going to get on with your authors and get the best out of them.

In a large publishing company, the control and administrative functions are carried out by senior managers who determine strategic goals, set targets and monitor production, sales and the functioning of the organization. While some have specialist roles in finance, legal affairs or human resources, the core of senior management is usually made up of one or more managing editors who have direct previous experience of creative work in publishing. Some will operate from a perspective which understands and encourages the autonomy and self-managing characteristics of the creative work process. Others, however, taking a more 'managerialist' stance, will be the source of tension with editorial staff who value their autonomy, nonconformity and indeterminacy.

Recorded music

As in most other creative sectors, the popular music industry has a diverse range of organizations, including both large-scale international companies and small, 'independent' businesses. However, they are closely linked and the problems of job design and work organization are essentially the same across the sector. The largest companies have a divisional structure which resembles the shape of other large bureaucratic organizations, with the functions of general management, financial management, human resources management and marketing in much the same form as elsewhere. In a small company the same functions will exist but will be combined into one or a few roles. Strategy and managerial leadership is often closely linked with the marketing function because of the music industry's need to closely monitor cultural trends and market shifts. Where musical genres and patterns of tasks are well established and predictable, it is of course possible to apply methods to production and marketing which approximate quite closely to the bureaucratic model. However, the dynamics of popular musical culture require organizations to have the means to incorporate subjective judgements about culture, taste and artists' potential into the decision-making process. This is achieved primarily through the role of an A & R (artist and repertoire) director, a senior management position, although it is likely to be occupied by a relatively youthful manager with previous experience of the 'creative' side of the industry. Senior management can thus remain in touch with rapidly changing markets and can sustain an ethos of continuous cultural innovation and entrepreneurialism at the core of the organization.

The A & R management role is inherently dualistic, involving an affinity with musical culture as well as strong commitment to commercial priorities. The twin functions are described by one such manager in a large record company as follows:

> One, which is the most familiar, is the talent acquisition side of it. The A & R department is responsible for attracting artists and signing artists to the record label and maintaining the balance of the artists' roster. And also the other function of the job is to oversee your apportioned part of that artist's roster – oversee them both creatively and try to develop them songwriting wise, recording wise, touring – just the whole image, the whole package of an artist. Helping to develop the new and developing acts that you sign and turn them into a successful artist. That requires not only a creative vision of where that artist is going but an understanding of the marketing process behind the record and also a deep understanding of the financials involved in terms of the recording and touring and the effect that has on the company's profit line.

A handful of key individuals cannot, however, be expected to have detailed knowledge of all areas of the market. The typical strategy for maintaining contact with trends is to acquire or buy into existing small companies that have already identified the market:

> If . . . you're so obsessed with your own little trendy area you are ultimately not very good at your job. There are plenty of labels who do cater for a very specialist audience and for a company [of our] size it's probably far more beneficial for us to go out and acquire those companies, and have all their marketing skills and know-how up and running, rather than let one individual determine the artists' roster by their particular taste.

The A & R function is therefore the key interface between commerce and culture in the music business, the point at which cultural judgements are converted into business decisions and vice versa (Negus, 1996). The creative work process (as such performance, recording, product design and marketing) involves a wide range of artistic, technical and organizational skills which can be combined in a variety of ways in different settings. While it is quite possible for all aspects of record production to be carried out 'in-house' according to a functional division of labour, there is an increasing tendency to externalize activities, and to use a complex network of independent professional specialists in talent scouting, record producing, managing bands or promotion. The aim of such arrangements is to minimize costs, maintain flexibility and spread risks as widely as possible. The result is a creative work process which is complex, network-based and built around short-term contracts. Technical expertise in sound recording for example, or craft qualifications in music composition or performance, combined with practical experience, are the normal conditions for entry to the business, but occupational categories are loosely defined and individual 'careers' typically involve overlap or movement between categories.

Advertising

In the advertising sector, company organization is also in three distinct parts which again reflect the same functional distinctions between control and coordination, creative roles, and production tasks. In fact, the advertising industry is one which regularly uses the term 'creative' to describe the group of staff who have the main responsibility for interpreting the client's brief. Employees in a typical creative advertising agency are divided into three main groups: the account group, the creative group and the media group respectively.[1] Work in the account group is led by an account manager and is focused on the relationship between the agency and the client. The tasks include developing an advertising strategy, project planning, creating advertisements, placing them and monitoring their effectiveness. The relationship with the client – essential for understanding and interpreting their needs – means that there is a premium on interpersonal communication skills, and the ability to motivate a team. These tasks of leadership, control and coordination are essentially 'managerial' and some, such as market monitoring, are relatively routine and repetitive. However, the skills involved are those of organizing a diverse set of activities which cannot be reduced to a predefined set of rules and procedures. This is best illustrated by the activities at the core of the creative work process. The creative team typically comprises as a minimum an art director and copywriter, responsible for visuals and words respectively. In a larger organization, the team may include staff with related but more junior roles, plus a television producer in the case of film and TV advertising, and others with specialist skills in typography, graphics, animation, etc. The art director is likely to be qualified in graphic design and to have a great deal of autonomy or 'artistic freedom' to try out ideas, experiment, and indulge in lateral thinking. The remaining tasks of production are carried out by the media planning group, which is orientated towards market research, purchasing media time and space, and scheduling expenditure.

The organization of a large agency is likely to take into account the need for continuity and cohesion in work teams. Thus, for example, one agency has five different groups and under each group head there are about ten or twelve accounts or projects. An account director described the structure as 'like a mini-agency within a big agency. And you tend to have all of your accounts within that group as much as possible . . . But it's certainly not exclusive. I mean, the groups are not competitive. They're not run on a sort of a profit motivation.' But the boundaries of the division of labour reflect the tension between creative and business priorities. An agency managing director commented:

> It's a slightly naive stereotype, but broadly speaking most creative people don't like planners because they think planners stop their work getting seen. [The Planning Director] will say that what planners do is stop the turkeys getting out. Creative people actually, for the most part, don't have very good judgement about their own work.

Alternatively, small agencies may be created, according to a similar logic, as independent entities, where some of these tensions are resolved.

There is a considerable diversity of types of organizations in advertising. The largest national and international agencies cater for all forms of media and provide a full range of services to a variety of clients. Others are relatively small and either specialize in a particular type of client or offer a specialized service in one of the above areas of activity. In large as well as small organizations there is an unusually rapid turnover of structures, teams, personnel and types of activity as each company attempts to maintain and develop the creative depth which is so closely linked with their commercial success. Advertising agencies are particularly interesting from the organizational point of view because they combine a very strong commercial orientation with highly indeterminate cultural work in terms of image creation and copywriting. Like other creative roles in different media sectors, but to an even greater extent, the creative in advertising is defined not by qualifications or position in the organization but rather by their portfolio of work and achievements. Success can bring rapid advancement either within an agency or through spiralling moves to other agencies.

The performing arts

The organization of work in the performing arts is heavily influenced by the project nature of productions. While there is of course some continuity in the management of theatres, opera houses and concert halls, as well as in the activities connected with finance, publicity and ticket sales, and front of house, each production involves a unique combination of roles and activities. The basic 'production' roles are the performers (actors, dancers, musicians) and those who construct the setting (stage design, construction, lighting, sound). The producer/director plays the key role in combining these contributions. Performing arts production is normally perceived as an artistic activity but leadership in the creative work process means that the producer/director is also required to interpret the work – be it a play, opera, ballet or show – in the light of various conditions and constraints including finance, the limits of the venue, the nature of the audience and so forth. It is therefore a combined managerial and creative role.

Management of the performing arts has also had a dual character shaped by the differences between the activities funded from the public purse and those in the commercial sector. Management of the former has traditionally taken the form of administration of budgets, with performance being measured by the evaluation of professional-based reference groups, critics and audiences. However, with the erosion of public subsidies, the organization and culture of subsidized theatre, opera and ballet companies has been changing towards a system of management accounting based more strictly on cost centres, performance measures and more precise information systems. However, even from a finance director's point of view, there is a difference between performing arts and other sectors:

> There is a paradox here, isn't there, because I argue on the one hand management techniques in this industry are no different whatsoever and standard financial techniques are as relevant here as in any commercial setting. What is different is that the overall objective of this organization is not simply to generate profits for shareholders. It's a dual one of on the one hand, ensuring financial stability over time to achieve the artistic goals of the organization. It makes life much more interesting.

Those activities which can be measured – such as box office transactions – use modern communications and information technology and are highly routinized. Other activities are less amenable to financial management or control but in the commercial theatre, in particular, the decision to close a show or extend a run will be driven entirely by financial consideration rather than the show's critical reception. Advance publicity and promotion are also used in a highly calculative way to create the conditions for commercial success. In some of the performing arts, creative functions continue to play a leading role in artistic policy (for example, regularly to include new and less popular works in the repertoire) and can still override more immediate financial considerations. In practice many performing arts activities receive some form of subsidy or sponsorship, and are therefore hybrid in character. This is significant from the point of view of work organization and creativity because it tends to enlarge the area of autonomy which participants have and underpins the indeterminacy that is one of the hallmarks of the creative process. However, the opportunity provided by this form of support may also be a constraint if strings are attached.[2]

Strategy, control and creativity

This review of the typical divisions of labour and the organization of work across a range of creative industries has emphasized the parallels and common features of the creative work process. Thus, the titles of producer, editor, creative director or A & R director all represent jobs at the crucial interface between management and creative production. Holders of these titles are rarely called managers but they are a key element in the system of managerial control and coordination. Occupants of each of these roles experience a similar tension between the commercial and instrumental logic of running the business and the generation of new cultural forms in a context of uncertainty. If the paradox of creativity and control could be resolved with a single set of organizational principles or a standard formula it would be a simple matter to identify the tasks and apply the optimal solution. In practice, the paradox is a genuine one and what looks like a solution from one perspective creates a new set of problems from another. The remaining part of this chapter is a discussion of some of the most significant organizational strategies for maximizing both control and creativity. While they may appear to be industry-specific or linked with particular technologies or types of production, they are in fact general strategies which can be applied in the context of any creative industry, and usually have been.

The first strategy is one of division: it creates a line of *demarcation* between 'creatives' and others through job titles, responsibilities and working practices which attempt to show clearly where creative work ends and management begins. It is based on the notion that the best way to maximize the potential of creative people is to set the task and then extend to them the necessary autonomy for its execution. It is a strategy which is most clearly evident in the large-scale, vertically integrated type of organization which contains separate creative departments and a stratum of independent, professional workers whose activities are characterized by a very high level of autonomy, nonconformity and indeterminacy. The classic example of this strategy is the cultural bureaucracy of the BBC of the 1960s and 1970s. However, it is found in other settings ranging from the publicly subsidized performing arts and some family-owned publishing houses. In the case of the BBC, it was a strategy associated with what many regard as the 'golden age' of British television broadcasting because of the high quality of output and sustained record of innovation. In his account of work and careers at the BBC at this time, Burns shows how the identity of this key group of creative employees was shaped by a particular understanding and use of the concept of 'professional' (1977: 125). The occupations in broadcasting such as television producer or editor are not 'professions' in the classic sense of being based on expert knowledge, formal training and qualifications, restricted entry, independent status and an ethical code (Johnson, 1972; Burrage and Torstendahl, 1990). Instead, as mentioned above, the television producer typically has a high level of general, but not job- or task-specific, education combined with practical experience in relevant areas. The concept of professionalism which developed in the BBC during the 1960s was therefore a way of expressing the autonomous, indeterminate and non-conformist nature of the creative role in relation to other aspects of the organization. The professional in this sense is the person who can be relied on to perform the task without supervision, make independent judgements and accept the responsibility for them, and embody the values and culture of the organization. Professionals are not necessarily hostile to bureaucracy as many have argued. The strongly bounded division of labour is not, necessarily, a symptom of weakness or conflict in the organization. Rather, it is an outcome and expression of a unitary culture in which all activities take place 'in-house'; the different spheres of activity having their own forms of social relationship, authority and social control. The strategy of allowing creative workers to operate freely within a well-defined space in an enabling managerial culture is likely to be most successful when the organization is growing, when its financial position is secure, when good recruits are plentiful and when there is a strong demand for its products. This was certainly the case in the BBC of the 1960s and 1970s but not in the more recent period. Indeed, the lines of demarcation between managerial and production tasks have been eroded since the Corporation embarked on restructuring in order to reduce costs and prepare itself for more intense national and global competition. The strength of demarcation, however, is that it recognizes and protects autonomy, legitimates nonconformity and allows for indeterminacy in a well-defined organizational space.

The second strategy is well illustrated by recent changes in broadcasting but it also applies in large-scale commercial organizations which have well-elaborated functional divisions and a quasi-bureaucratic system of managerial control. The strategy is one of *incorporation*, namely, the absorption of key creative roles into the management structure itself. The process does not necessarily involve a change of titles but the producer, editor, creative or A & R director actually becomes an executive, and is thereby engaged directly and formally in managerial tasks which previously would have been carried out by a former creative or specialist manager. Examples of this type of 'incorporation' are the roles of the senior editors in a publishing house; the A & R director of a large music company; divisional heads or senior producers in broadcasting. They differ from the independent professionals described in the former strategy because they are directly answerable for commercial results as well as for cultural performance and they are identified with the company through their managerial staff position, which is usually a longer term contract than for creatives. Incorporation is most likely to occur in those sectors of activity where production is geared to large and relatively well-developed markets and where media products can be standardized, so that production and managerial control begin to approximate to the bureaucratic model. For example, in the music and film industries, markets are divided into styles and genres. For some of these markets, including those based on the exploitation of catalogues of old recordings, it is possible to remove much of the uncertainty which surrounds the development of new artists and recordings. Similarly, in some areas of book publishing like textbooks, manuals or reference series it is possible to plan for standardized output on the basis of stable patterns of demand. The key advantage of the incorporation of the creative process into the rationalized methods of management is the significant increase in control which it brings. Performance which would otherwise be assessed by subjective criteria is linked instead to the explicit calculation of quotas, costs and time. According to this strategy, the main gains are those of any efficient bureaucracy; that is, precise goals, clear unambiguous procedures and predictable outcomes.

There are, of course, limits to how far the bureaucratic model can be applied, which is the reason why it is not universally adopted and why it is resisted – at least by many creative workers. Incorporation implies a loss of autonomy and a restriction on the freedom to invent new solutions to the creative process. At the same time, indeterminacy is minimized. This is likely to have an impact on morale and motivation as creative workers find that managerial priorities erode their autonomous professional identity. In organizations with a very strong commercial orientation, such as international advertising agencies or publishing conglomerates, the prospect of career advancement through the organization or higher financial rewards may be sufficient to offset the loss of autonomy. Where the culture of the organization was originally public service-oriented – as in the BBC – the adjustment to a more incorporated style of creativity management is likely to be a difficult one for many employees. Professionals accept the culture of the organization as a necessary condition of working rather than as a source of values to which they personally subscribe.

The third strategy for resolving the paradoxical relationship between creativity and control is the *clustering* of organizations of different types. Instead of a line of demarcation within a unitary or vertically integrated organization, the activities of managerial control and the creative work process are separated out into distinct units. These are sub-contractors, often known as independents, although the latter term is misleading. They can have a variety of different forms of ownership or contractual arrangements with 'controlling' companies. The most striking example is the rise of independent television companies in the UK with the establishment of Channel 4 and the independent production quotas subsequently imposed on the rest of the industry. A significant proportion of television programme production now takes place outside the BBC and ITV companies in small and medium-sized firms which specialize in particular types of programme making. Other firms make specialized provision in equipment, post-production and other services. The result is a highly complex network of organizations of different types which combine, break up and recombine according to the needs of specific projects. The creative process is similarly complex and does not have a simple standard form. However, the most typical way for managerial and creative roles to be organized in smaller scale independent organizations is for them to be combined in the same person: for example, the independent producer who is also the owner and manager of a small production company. Such firms are often created by individuals who seek to recreate the conditions of autonomy, indeterminacy and nonconformity which once existed in the framework of cultural bureaucracies but which have since been eroded. However, the combination of roles and interlinked organizations presents its own problems. Autonomy to define and shape the creative work process is often associated with high levels of insecurity. Many small firms do not attract sufficient business to survive, or trade only intermittently. On the other hand, success also brings its problems. The independent producer whose company is growing has to balance the time spent on finance, contracts and administration with the demands of the creative process. Similar organizational structures and their associated tensions are found in the music industry and publishing, where many of the risks associated with innovation, pioneering trends, and niche markets are carried by smaller companies which are better placed to motivate their creative workers and be responsive to unpredictable changes in taste and fashion.

The fourth strategy represents the most radical way of resolving the organizational control/creativity paradox. It is a strategy of *segregating* the two elements, and is in fact the normal method of organizing the 'most' creative cultural workers such as novelists, scriptwriters, fine artists, actors, composers and musicians. The majority, if not all, of the workers in these categories are freelance because of the highly autonomous nature of the creative process and the difficulty of providing any structure of work organization and control other than that imposed by the individual creator himself or herself. Such is the extent of the segregation that freelance workers may require agents to bridge the gap between their sphere of creativity and the organizations which purchase their products or services. Segregation does not necessarily mean a hostile or conflictual relationship between freelance workers and the purchasing organizations, nor does it mean an absence of control as such. Creative workers have a maximum of autonomy in terms of control over their work process but they must also enter into highly structured contractual arrangements which specify content, formats, delivery dates and financial reward. Thus, according to this strategy of segregation, the dynamic of control and creativity does not disappear but simply adopts another form. From the managerial point of view, in large media organizations, the use of freelance workers has a number of distinct advantages. First, the risks in areas of high uncertainty in the creative process are distanced from the core. Products and services are purchased only as and when required. Second, there is greater flexibility in using freelance workers than permanent employees; if there is a sufficient supply it can be more closely matched to demand. The third advantage is that both freelancers and those who purchase their services each specialize in what they do best. The disadvantages of the segregation of functions are the vulnerability of creative workers to market fluctuations on the one hand, and, for contractors, the difficulty of monitoring, controlling and assuring the outcome of the creative work process.

These four 'ideal types' of the strategies for resolving the organizational paradox of *creativity* and *control* are not descriptions of actual companies or structures. The above illustrations simply highlight some of the relevant trends, but in practice, evidence of each of the strategies can be found in all the main sectors.

There are no complete, long-term solutions to this organizational paradox. One general conclusion which can be drawn, however, is that although organizational structures are changing and highly variable, creativity is an inherently social process which inevitably requires mediation through institutional structures of one kind or another. Without this, creativity fails to become a productive social process. The following chapters take up this theme according to a conceptual scheme that enables the issues to be explored in various organizational settings.

Notes

1 This discussion relates mainly to the 'creative' rather than the 'media' type of agency. See Chapter 2 p. 46 for a definition of this distinction. As mentioned, there is a growing tendency for specialization along these lines. However, it has been noted that there are implications for the creative process. Rupert Howell, in his inaugural speech as President of the Institute of Practitioners of Advertising, pointed out that there is 'a generation of media people who never directly experienced the process of producing good creative ideas, and similarly, a generation of planners and creatives whose only experience of the media is their own consumption of it' (13 April 1999).
2 Concern about spending on the arts, like other forms of public spending, has led to the creation of a new agency, Quest: the Quality, Efficiency and Standards Team. This body audits government-funded arts organizations and has wide-ranging powers to investigate their activities, monitor accounts and interview administrators to ensure they are reaching efficiency targets.

4

MANAGING CREATIVE ORGANIZATIONAL CULTURES

The ways of organizing creative production described in the previous chapter are closely linked with different management styles. Together, divisions of labour and management practices combine to create 'organizational culture'. This includes the formal and informal systems of action and meaning which make organization possible. Whereas in some sectors there are managerial attempts to impose tight forms of bureaucratic control, in others there is the recognition that those engaged within creative processes require degrees of autonomy whereby they are able to produce cultural products with a maximum of discretion and flexibility. When, for example, the cultural output can be standardized in terms of content, format and sequence, work activities can be made highly routine according to explicit procedures. On the other hand, there are sectors of the media which are more likely to be focused on 'one-off' projects which, because of their specific requirements in terms of organization and delivery, do not lend themselves to the same degree of routinization. An example of the former is commercial radio broadcasting which is highly structured according to clearly defined routines, while film production or open-air musical events may be cited as illustrations of the latter.

This chapter continues to draw on evidence from interviews

with managers and creative employees in order to examine the relationship between styles of management and different organizational cultures.[1] As a working definition it can be said that organizational culture is the pattern (regular or irregular, stable or changing) of guiding assumption, principles, ideas, values, and rules of behaviour which members of the organization have. It may be well defined or very fluid; it may be shared by most members of the organization or there may be significant differences between them. The culture of an organization may be consciously articulated or simply taken for granted. Whichever form it takes, an organizational culture is the result of the active involvement of members in the definition of tasks, the negotiation of roles, and the use of organizational mechanisms to influence outcomes. One of the advantages of using this concept is that it opens up to scrutiny the 'official' versions of company aims, policy and organization and, as often as not, challenges them.

The limits to bureaucracy

As a first step towards understanding different management styles, it is appropriate to ask the question: does the concept of 'bureaucracy' have any meaning in the culture of creative organizations? In Chapter 1 it was introduced as a limiting case or ideal type of management and organization through our discussion of theory but does it have a similar meaning in the real world of organizations? In fact, 'bureaucracy' is used spontaneously by many respondents in the course of the interviews, though not with great frequency. Its carries connotations which are more negative than positive, because bureaucratic forms and procedures are generally seen as inappropriate for controlling creative tasks. There is, nonetheless, some recognition of the need for formal procedures to govern some aspects of organization. For example, an Assistant Floor Manager working in BBC Drama illustrates the way in which the bureaucratic aspects of organization in a large, hierarchical and publicly accountable organization impose a formal framework – literally by means of a 'book of rules'. In practice, however, the nature of the work does not permit constant recourse to fixed rules, they must become part of an intuitive pattern of behaviour and be followed in spirit rather than according to the letter:

> *Assistant Floor Manager:* There is a book about an inch thick which is the AFM's guide, which explains everything that you are required to do but . . . you do none of it and you do all of it, there really is very little boundary as to what I could be asked to do and have to do. It's basically, you know, at the end of it all the contract says 'and to assist the production in the best way possible as directed', so . . .
> *Interviewer:* Have you read that Bible, as it were?
> *Assistant Floor Manager:* I have, but most of it does not apply in any particular job. It applies to all of it, to all the AFM's jobs: working in the studio and working on location are completely different things so half of it immediately I can ignore . . . and it's very very, not bureaucratic, that's the wrong word – detailed, and a lot of it just you do not need to do. Some of it's useful but it's, basically it's a job that requires a lot of common sense and some knowledge of how the BBC works because it's, being very departmental-ized you have to know who to ask to get permission from.

The expression 'doing none of it or all of it' captures the high degree of indeterminacy and autonomy which is typical of creative work tasks. It does not suggest that there is such a high level of nonconformity. Rather, it indicates the extent to which a cultural bureaucracy encourages the creative worker to identify with the organization in order to minimize the risks as well as maximize the benefits associated with indeterminate and autonomous roles.

A sense of organizational identity comes from seeing one's role within the wider organizational context and division of labour. This, as well as an occupational identity, is evidence of integration into the organizational culture and involves recognizing that organizations are complex and that they must perform a variety of activities. While there is a common perception of the BBC as the epitome of a bureaucratic organization, and while in some cases it is regarded as an unsympathetic context for creative work, the most common perception – as in the above quotation – is that bureaucratic forms have their place, even in relation to creative work. The most frequent synonym for bureaucracy in the interviews is 'administration', a term for those organizational tasks which are governed by legal or financial procedures, including personnel, health and safety, copyright, accountancy. They are viewed as separate but unavoidable tasks, a necessary evil and means to an end ideally performed by specialists in order for creative employees to execute their tasks. While it is recognized that there is a danger that rounds of meetings, trails of memos, and written instructions (like the *Producers' Guidelines*) can become sterile and disconnected from the real tasks of production, they are tolerated in the interest of good communications, accountability and compliance with public regulations. But they are not accepted as an intrinsic part of professional creative activity. The metaphors of bureaucratic systems reflect this: 'them and us' or the 'inverted pyramid' image used by the television drama producer quoted earlier. A chief executive in a music company echoes the same theme: 'It is a constant . . . you have to have legal and business affairs, you have to have human resources, you have to have finance; you can't not have those things, and then you may have these other [creative] areas.' Bureaucracy is experienced as a something separate, an external force.

Among some managers, however, and especially those working in small-scale independent organizations in television, publishing and music, there is much greater hostility towards layers of administration which are not directly connected with creative work. They are seen as a real impediment because they are a source of delay in taking decisions, they complicate the lines of responsibility, and they dilute creative judgements. The images are far more critical: 'geriatric management' and 'good bureaucrats' who are 'brain-dead' (both comments from independent television). The director of a small publishing house said: 'You can't bureaucratize, you can't have rules and regulations and procedures, you can't issue memos, you can't sit behind the desk and give instructions to either editors, authors, or whatever – it's about newness and innovation.' These same critics are individuals who have often shown great skill in the organization of small to medium-sized companies over a number of years, following their deliberate departure from large corporations. They are strongly inclined to view administration as a set of activities which can be most effectively carried out in small organizations with a strong culture of personal interaction. The organization is tightly controlled by an individual or members of a small management team who are in a position to make independent and rapid decisions. It is noteworthy that in the interviews in advertising agencies there were no spontaneous references to bureaucracy or bureaucratic forms of management. The concept, if not the reality, of administration through rational procedures was simply not part of the everyday vocabulary in these settings.

There is an alternative, more positive, view expressed by those in radio broadcasting. The chief executive of a radio station held that the disciplines of management and administration are not only a necessary means to get work done but also a *constructive* form of discipline:

> You have a bunch of people like me wandering around in suits trying to make a profit and run a business and look after the people and the shareholders and all that stuff, and that requires a certain amount of kind of corporate discipline about it, budgets have to be adhered to and procedures and health and safety and all those sorts of things are very important in a company like this. And then you've got a bunch of people who are much more concerned with music and entertainment and humour and all those sorts of things, and when the two worlds collide they can make for both an extremely exciting and invigorating kind of atmosphere and it also has a kind of tension between those two worlds, and I think it makes for a very very interesting place to work as a result. I don't see it as being a handicap in the business at all. I personally find it extremely stimulating, but there again I came from a production background so I have a natural affinity with that side of the business, but I think that an environment whereby you have people pursuing the goals of corporate discipline and management alongside people who have a mission to entertain I think, has more benefits to both sides than it does disadvantages.

Thus, there are several interpretations of bureaucracy which emphasize, respectively, its inevitability, negativity and utility. They are not separate or restricted to particular creative sectors.

They are found in combination or in succession – as in the case of a book publishing company which started out as an autocratically structured organization under the strict control of the founder, became a conglomerate-owned operation which adopted a hands-off approach, and then transformed into a bureaucratically controlled and highly coordinated international multinational described by a former manager as 'obsessed with structure and charts showing who reported to whom, and who was at the end of which dotted line'. Indeed, the three perspectives on the 'bureaucratic' aspects of management are present across all sectors of the creative industries, and because the burden of administration is a commonly occurring theme, they are a useful indicator of the control and cohesion within organizational cultures. They show that within some companies there are compromises between formal systems of managerial control and the autonomy of creative employees which take different forms according to the size of the organization, the type of creative activity, and the style of entrepreneurship. The limits to bureaucracy in a creative context are clearly visible in the formation of new, network organizations, often designed as an 'escape' from the dulling effects of the large cultural or commercial bureaucracy. They can also be seen in the measure to which larger companies extend a significant degree of autonomy to categories of employees who are most closely associated with processes of cultural production. The next section will explore the impact of disciplines of control – especially financial control through budgets, accounting and financial reporting – which managers in all types of organizations use to structure and rationalize creative activities.

⟨ Mechanisms of control ⟩

The formal responsibility for managerial control obviously rests with those in recognized managerial positions. However, in media settings it is unusual for these positions and responsibilities to be explicitly and clearly defined, even in large organizations such as the BBC. The reasons for this are closely related to the indeterminacy of creative tasks and the non-routine features of the production process. However, managers must still have a role in coordinating and controlling activities according to priorities set by the organization, its shareholders or other bodies to which it is accountable. In practice, these priorities are established through a combination of organizational and financial mechanisms. Organizational structures are an expression of the system of power and its distribution among organization members. The tendency in creative organizations is for there to be a substantial devolution of responsibilities as well as for creative and 'non-interventionist' styles of managerial behaviour. Thus the chief executive of a group of independent radio stations compared the management of broadcasting with manufacturing:

> I'm not sure that you could just take management as a line management skill and take somebody who'd run a very good motor car plant and put them into running a radio station or a television station. I think one ends up probably, as much a leader as a manager in broadcasting. In that you really have to devolve much more control, I think, although I speak with little experience of outside organizations, much more control, than would be thought normal.

From a management point of view, the main benefit of devolution is to move decision making to the level(s) where relevant information is most readily available, to enhance motivation and self-responsibility, and to improve accountability. These ideals correspond closely with the views of autonomous professionals as far as aesthetic judgements are concerned, because they regard creative work as a personal responsibility. However, when devolution also includes a responsibility for budgeting, scheduling work, planning and administration, it is often perceived as an unwelcome tightening of control, an excuse for more bureaucratic intervention, and an unwelcome addition to an already full workload. Significant moves towards greater devolution, such as occurred in the BBC during the 1990s, always involve a transformation of organizational culture and increase the likelihood of divergent perceptions of the organization. The 'ideal' solution is one where control over the output of creative activities coincides with control over spending and vice versa, but the correspondence is rarely exact. The following scenario, described by a department head in BBC radio drama, is more common. There is clearly a high level of trust between 'managers' and creative professionals, supported by the fact that managers have typically emerged from a production background themselves:

> It's a sort of controlling and a managing role as well as an editorial role. I decide the editorial flavour and then I check that there's enough money to pay for it. Then I'll schedule the play and I'll check that the producer is promoting it. The actual business of casting and producing the play is for the producer to do. The producer goes there, does that, with some reference to me, if I've previously asked for it.

⟨Management can improve control within a devolved system, for example by establishing ground rules for procedure. In the context cited above, there was a rule that dramas should only be bought if they had a producer attached to them. This meant that producers not only had a direct responsibility for finding new 'products' but also for considering their costs and financial implications. Prior to this, producers were perceived to have had greater freedom and were less likely to be involved in negotiations with management over detailed budgets. However, even with devolved responsibility managers resisted the idea of 'having power' and preferred to talk of management by walking around, allowing people to work for themselves, and adopting a 'hands-off' style. One of the characteristics of most devolved systems is that control can still be applied after the event, through performance review, reporting procedures and budget monitoring. Thus, the disciplines of a reduction in the budget, downgrading to low-status production, or the ultimate sanction of dismissal, can all be applied following retrospective judgements.⟩

The workings of financial control mechanisms, and the limits they can come up against in a creative context, are well illustrated by book publishing (Coser *et al.*, 1981). Books are individual commodities which have value as intellectual property but they also have production costs and overheads, and they must make a specific contribution to profits. In principle at least, the performance of each book can be tracked at frequent intervals and can be combined with the performance of other titles to assess the contribution which an editor or a department is making to the company's overall financial performance. Aided by computer systems which combine information from all relevant sources, companies can make most reporting operations both accurate and routine. How effective, then, are these mechanisms as forms of control, and how do they relate to forms of organizational culture? Basic accounting, concerned with income and expenditure, paying bills and salaries, and costing overheads, is likely to be based on standard systems. The things which make publishing different from, say, a manufacturing operation are the sale or return system, complex contracts and royalty payment to authors, and the uncertain timescale between commissioning, delivery and production. The publisher acquires a volume of rights for each particular 'product' which is marketed throughout the world. There are rights for paperback, serialization and sometimes film options. These create complex accounting problems shaped by possibly thousands of subtly different individual contracts. As a response to these complexities, publishers will set basic parameters for volume and timing of publications, according to the financial and creative profiles of the company. This is described by an accountant in a successful 'independent' publishing company as follows:

> I set basically parameters for what we can afford to spend during the course of the financial year . . . That then determines essentially how many books we are going to publish in a year, therefore how many titles we need to acquire this year for next year. And there is an overall figure which is applied to that. You then break that figure down into categories of books so that we can determine how many fiction books we want to buy, how many biographies, current affairs, reference books, and so on. We will further subdivide those categories into major books, minor books, if you like, and the run-of-the-mill books, I suppose. And we will therefore know that we need to acquire, say, ten major books in the course of the year, twenty of the next category and the majority of the books in the bottom category. Therefore the editors know what their targets are and then I monitor them as the books are bought.

Each book or category therefore has a measurable payback which can be compared with standard performance criteria. In the light of this information, management can takes steps to reprint, promote particular titles more vigorously, dispose of stock, etc. With

increasing competition between publishers and shorter production cycles it is increasingly important for firms to have these
detailed monitoring systems. However, as one publishing managing director said, speaking of comparisons between publishing
and other businesses: 'It may be a bit similar to IBM – this business
is profit-driven as is IBM, but the difference is that you only make
profit by getting the other things right.' He, like many other
managers in the creative sector, refers to it as a 'people business'
and to the need to be obsessed with the product as well as with
the financial figures. The use of financial reporting to monitor
and control the performance of creative employees is therefore
tempered by a consideration for their creative judgement, their
'instincts', their knowledge of specific markets, and even their
type of personality. Another publishing manager said:

> You have to understand that I have a kind of stable of
> thoroughbreds here and if I treated them like junior accoun-
> tants, they'd all tell me to piss off. The interesting part of my
> job is trying to harness the efforts of people, some of whose
> first priority in life is the art product and mart, and so to be
> here at all they all have to have made a financial impact in
> their previous sales figures . . . [My relationship with editors
> is] riddled with respect for them, rather than a kind of boss
> and boy relationship, and I try very hard to understand
> things that they understand perhaps more about than I do,
> such as keeping the image of the firm alive in the literary
> world. There's this phenomenon about publishing a book
> which gets brilliant reviews, but doesn't sell any copies, but
> the whole world associates you with this book and if you
> were to entirely exclude that sort of book, you would be a
> different company to the one we are trying to be, which is at
> the forefront of quality publishing.

There is clearly a significant subjective element even in the most
rigorous financial appraisal and these major decisions typically
involve both commercial and creative judgements. Editors speak
of 'gut feeling' or 'just knowing that something is absolutely terrific' and discuss these feelings in editorial meetings. But of course
they are not entirely arbitrary or purely subjective. For example,
while the judgement that a children's book will sell steadily for ten

years involves a different equation from the one which predicts an initial subscription of 200,000 copies for a novel, they both build on similar combinations of knowledge, experience and rational appraisal as well as risk. These are indications that the autonomy and indeterminacy in the work of creative employees is still a valued part of the organizational culture of publishing.

There is a different type of organizational culture with other mechanisms of control in the performing arts, where management tends to have a project focus around a particular play, performance, show or exhibition. Financial and general managers become more directly involved in projects as part of a management team and their recommendations and decisions are likely to have a more direct impact on production. The financial director of a national theatre company, which is an organization with a publicly appointed board and a responsibility to produce plays according the highest artistic standards, illustrates this:

> I think it's an absolutely vital part of the job to make things happen and to try as best as one can to provide the resources to fulfil the artistic programme over a period of time. That often means saying no. I am very lucky to have colleagues who understand there are very necessary roles that have to be played, not just in finance but also by the technical people and that the whole producing process has to be healthy in this organization. For an artistic organization like this to flourish, you've got to have that essential balance working healthily between art artistically and materially . . . We are all involved as much in art as money.

His language echoes the artistic aims of the organization as well as the vocabulary of cost measurement and financial control systems. Motivation comes from the critical success and reputation of the theatre as much as from commercial success, and from what he describes as the 'integrity' of the organizational culture:

> It is very much that people appreciate the integrity. The fact that decisions are not taken to achieve just profit. I think people respond to that. I think if there is integrity in what is being planned and it is successful it gives people a sense that management has integrity in all its other dealings with staff –

it will treat them well and value what they do and make them feel they are making a contribution. They feel very much wanted as part of a team. You feel good about working for an organization which is exceedingly successful.

The general director of a national opera company describes its organizational culture in similar terms of 'single-mindedness', cohesion and management by 'instinct'. Provocatively, he says: 'There is no management; the management culture is false, it is a concept that is studied in management manuals and in business schools.' But what is important is 'direction':

By direction, I mean momentum towards a goal or ideal or both. If an organization or group of people are single-minded enough to have an ideal and out of that ideal fashion a series of goals and objectives that help realize that ideal, I think the institution they work in will have a kind of momentum, a kind of gravity that will reach that goal willy-nilly, partly because management success can only happen if that idea is very clear. I think in a place like an opera house, if it is to succeed, the goals have to be frighteningly clear because they are very complex institutions.

He defines the ideals in terms of the artistic aims and historic traditions of the opera company as well as the personal visions of its staff, namely that opera, although musically led, is a dramatic process of interpretation. It should have a concept of objective, musical quality supported by a dramatic conscience. It should be accessible to the widest possible variety of people and in a form that is of the highest possible quality. These aims do not in themselves imply a particular form of organizational design – hence certain differences between national operas in different countries – but neither do they imply that an organization of up to 1000 people with a very diverse range of activities can do without a structure. The largest of the UK opera companies shows quite the contrary. The Royal Opera House traditionally used a very hierarchical model of organization based on directorates with distinct functions, which a former general director described as pyramidal and like a 'naval ship' in character. According to this model, routine activities should run like clockwork and each level is answerable to the next. Each function is given as much freedom as possible provided it is consistent with the overall goals and aims of the organization.

The difference between this and a profit-making bureaucracy is in the criteria of performance. In the publicly subsidized arts, there is no unambiguous language for communicating performance or quantifiable measures such as earnings per share, profitability, or market share, which give good indicators of how a company is performing. The profit motive itself relates to clearly measurable criteria. In the public sector the nearest approximation to a profit motive is the aims described above which can be translated into the question 'Are you maximizing the output for a given input?' But there is no straightforward set of criteria for the answer, only a series of different measures, many of them qualitative. The finance director of one opera company commented with more than a hint of frustration that he didn't have a simple shorthand language for the discussion of 'value for money'. The mechanisms of organizational control and performance assessment, therefore, reflect this in the way they continue to emphasize a common culture, commitment to an overriding goal, high levels of trust within teams, and autonomous working within a structured system. The organizational culture resembles a cultural bureaucracy model with the additional feature that output is, by definition, project-based and the majority of creative employees are brought together on short-term contracts or as freelancers. As the publicly subsidized arts sector encounters grant reductions, seeks commercial sponsorship and faces fiercer competition, there is a growing tendency for organizations to strengthen their financial functions, and to create special departments for marketing, merchandizing, sponsorship and commercial operations. To this extent, they are moving towards a model of a profit-driven bureaucracy.

Smaller organizations in the theatre and performing arts tend to operate with a 'small is beautiful' culture based on strong individual entrepreneurial skills, low overheads and good networking. A typical case is a three-person company (plus a part-time book-keeper) which runs a West End theatre. The managing director says:

I like to keep the operation small, I don't want to have a large overhead, because then you get into producing plays merely to get the producer's fee in order to keep the office going. And I don't want to do that, I'd rather have a very small office, very small personnel . . . last year I produced six plays in the West End of London out of these two rooms, and they all opened, there was no problem. I don't want to have a huge overhead. I mean, I have a long lease on this office.

In such cases, it is perhaps inappropriate to refer to an organizational culture as such, because the structuring of activities is in a constant state of flux, with production teams constantly brought together, disbanded and recomposed. The key to control and integration within these 'project teams' is the mutual dependency of autonomous 'creatives' for whom the theatrical production is the essential vehicle for their artistic talents. They identify with the 'theatre', not particular organizations or employers, and their reputations and earnings are made through the track record of their productions, reviews and audience response, but not through organizational careers.

Advertising agencies represent an interesting mix of organizational cultures which is largely dependent on their size. The largest will have several hundred employees working in a single location with a well-defined structure and procedures. These are represented in complex organizational charts and sets of guidelines resembling a typical bureaucracy. Thus, in the JWT agency, for example, staff reported a standard way of doing account planning, known as the 'Thompson Way', and 'The Account Manager's Handbook and Toolkit' which enshrines certain disciplines of thought that are applied across all departments. One account manager in the organization describes it as a 'very useful discipline . . . to ensure that there is some sort of consistency' across departments and between different management and creative activities. These elements of bureaucratic discipline are likely to be found in all larger companies and they help to account for the perception that creative employees are increasingly aware of the commercial priorities in the sector. But while they contribute to the integration of the organizational culture, they do not define it. Certain aspects of the process of advertising can be routinized but the core activity is based on the verbal and visual creativity nurtured in creative teams. The tensions which can arise within the organizational culture of larger agencies are described by the creative director of such a company:

I've often thought it's like not since the court of the Sun King have there been so – and I'm not an historian – have there been so many people of such different talents assembled in one building . . . It's very bad if you get fragmented groups of people . . . I once worked in an agency on eleven or twelve floors, and consequently you tend to get tremendous stratification. Some people never walk, other people are always peripatetic, you can't nail them down – where are they? Other people sit in their rooms and never move. That had a very bad effect on the agency's integration, like you would get planners thinking about isolated, empirical ideas, and often they would then hand them, polished like a Fabergé Egg, to the creative people, who are not as literate or as academic as them, and certainly not as elusive in their verbal thinking, and they wouldn't know what to do with this. So they would tend to put it on one side and start again. I find it better if you get the creative people, the planners and the account men rubbing sparks off each other, on a day-to-day basis. That means the creative work can define the strategy, and the strategy can refine the creative work, and vice versa.

The image of the creative team is typically one of high energy and hyperactivity: 'like an exploding universe', according to this creative director, where fission and fusion are both likely to be present. The skill of management is to allow the freedom and the facilities for creative ideas to form, but within a structure of deadlines, budget parameters and work schedules. At the micro-level, much depends on personalities and creative interaction between partners or small teams at the core of this process. The organizational culture must therefore acknowledge and support this if teams are to perform successfully. Even in large agencies, where functions and clients are well established and there is a predictability about the output, creative teams are formed and reformed at relatively frequent intervals, at least every one or two years. The mobility of staff is a reflection of the need to generate creative teams for new accounts and to provide job interest and career opportunities for creative employees. Their relationships are often so close as to be called 'marriages' and interaction between individuals may be quite idiosyncratic and noncon-formist. Personalities which would not mesh well in other types of organization are tolerated and even encouraged. In other words, there is recognition of the need to tolerate a work process charac-terized by autonomy, nonconformity and indeterminacy. A man-ager in a large agency identifies some of the typical features of the work process as being outside the usual sphere of rational calculation and pragmatic responses:

> To get to the top of the field as an art director or copywriter you have to be very good at generating advertising ideas, and that mentality does not by and large create someone who is good at management – of people or situations. And I simplis-tically put it down to that you need a sort of child-like curios-ity to do good advertising because you have to approach things with wonderment and a slight lateral sense and exclude all of the other extraneous influences. And that child-like curiosity actually means that you are in many ways child-like, so the throwing of toys metaphorically is part of your make-up, and it is quite hard to find an interest in the diplomacy side of management.

He contrasts this with the account manager as a type, who has to be 'totally pragmatic' and unemotional. The distinction is, of course, based on stereotypes of the main subcultures within the organization rather than hard and fast differences in personality traits. In reality, creative employees often become managers and do not experience a sudden personality change or culture shock. What happens is that the organization interprets itself in terms of generalized behaviour patterns in order to make the management of people more predictable by encouraging subcultures which reinforce appropriate working practices. As in other creative organizations, the major mechanism of management is more through the *culture* than through hands-on supervision of work and organizational tasks. The communication of these cultural norms is widespread across the advertising industry, encouraging

93

high levels of mobility between firms.[2] Creative employees in advertising require autonomy and they must be prepared to tolerate high levels of indeterminacy in their work roles. But they also need an awareness of the nature, purpose and scheduling of the production process as a whole – the 'media' as well as the 'creative' side of the business. This explains why some advertising agencies are among the largest and most centralized companies in the creative industries. But it also helps to account for creative employees who quit their jobs in these large companies and set up their own businesses or partnerships. They will perceive this to be a means whereby they can escape the constraints of bureaucracy and freely express their creativity for personally controlled profit-making purposes.

Conceptualizing organizational creativity

Drawing upon the above discussion, it is possible to explore the sources and patterns of organizational differentiation within the creative industries and bring some order to them. First, it is necessary to identify the principles according to which such differences may be determined and the outcomes for the design of creative companies. In analysing organizational structures, it is possible to specify two *axial principles*: that of *coordination* and that of *control*.[3] On the basis of these, four types of media organization may be described. More specifically, it enables us to describe the different ways according to which creativity, as a work process, is managed within different sectors of the media. It also helps us to track patterns of organizational restructuring as they respond to changes in the commercial and cultural environment.

The first axis relates to *coordination*, by which is meant the different mechanisms by which work activities are interrelated within a coherent and clearly defined division of labour. In traditional manufacturing industry, as well as within highly centralized forms of bureaucracy, there is often a precisely defined division of labour which is integrated through an explicit management process. Management defines the roles and responsibilities of occupational groups or project teams according to a set of interlocking functions, usually within a hierarchy. However, the extent to which work tasks are subdivided and the degree to which these are *coordinated* will be highly variable not only according to economic sectors but also between companies operating within the same spheres of activity. While the nature of both products and technology can predispose the subdivision of work into either highly specialized tasks or flexible, multiskilled practices, other influences may include custom and practice, manager–worker negotiations and senior management philosophy. The latter is sometimes overlooked but it is clearly significant because diverse organizational forms are found among companies utilizing similar technologies for the purpose of trading in particular products and services. Such organizations, therefore, can be either highly centralized or decentralized in terms of their coordinating mechanisms and decision-making processes. They may be either highly routinized and based on work tasks which are fragmented into specialized roles, or they may give priority to flexible working and loosely defined roles within multifunctional teams.

Thus, it is possible to differentiate between organizations according to the extent to which work processes are coordinated – by whatever means. This is important to emphasize, since the mechanisms of coordination could be through explicit rules and instructions from management but, equally, they can be based upon other processes. These include mutual adjustment among colleagues working within task-orientated terms, coordination through the systems of technology or software employed or, indeed, by the requirement to collaborate within a specific client-/customer-orientated project. Hence, coordinating mechanisms can be highly variable, ranging from a high degree of integration to an equally high degree of fragmentation. Within highly *integrated* organizations, there will be clearly defined aims and objectives, strongly held values to which the overwhelming majority of employees are bound, and work processes which, although diverse in their nature, are orientated to these values. In *fragmented* organizations, on the other hand, coordinating mechanisms are underdeveloped within the organization as a whole and there is the absence of clearly defined aims and objectives around which shared values can be developed. Alternatively, the aims and objectives may be naturally diffuse. Where these are 'cultural' (for example, public service, artistic integrity, or quality), coordination is more likely to be looser than in organizations which have strictly commercial aims. The fragmented nature of such organizations may be reflected in an excessive emphasis upon departmentalization, functional specialization or, more commonly in creative companies, projects.

Similarly, it is possible to differentiate between organizations in terms of their mechanisms of *control*. If the principle of coordination refers essentially to the system of linkages between organizational parts defined according to management aims and objectives, the control principle is concerned with the procedures and means whereby these results are achieved. Thus, the formal articulation of control mechanisms is particularly evident within bureaucratic organizations where operating mechanisms are explicitly stated in the form of rules, regulations and procedures. But this is only one of the types of mechanism of social control available in organizations. Through the application of the principles of scientific management, hierarchical control systems became almost synonymous with the industrial organization. Control is achieved by making individuals accountable to superordinates through clearly stipulated reporting processes. However, in creative organizations, organizational control may be exercised either explicitly through formal reporting mechanisms or more indirectly and implicitly via processes of mutual adjustment, self-managing work groups and collective decision making.

Thus, the application of the principles of coordination and control can have diverse outcomes for forms of organization design. This is particularly the case in the extent to which processes of coordination are centrally managed and work relations are directly controlled through hierarchical reporting procedures. When this is the case, the outcome is a form of bureaucracy of the sort described by Max Weber in his 'ideal type' formulation. As a result, there is a high degree of organizational integration in terms of structures, processes and culture. Compliant, conformist and role-orientated organizational behaviour is the likely outcome. On the other hand, the principle of coordination can be articulated according to a number of 'emergent' processes without central direction – as in the mutual adjustment found among professional, technical or expert staff collaborating on specific projects – or in the operation of networks. Instead of centralized bureaucratic forms of organization with clearly defined divisions of labour, the likely outcomes are structures and processes that give the appearance of fragmentation and diversity. In place of such corporate integrative mechanisms as shared culture and employee conformity through role compliance, such organizations are likely to be characterized by a diversity of operating practices and a variety of forms of employee behaviour. It is typical for many organizations in the creative industries to have reporting processes – beyond those within immediate work groups – that are ambiguously defined and, for most employees, irrelevant. In the absence of such mechanisms of organizational integration, the primary factor binding the individual to the organization or network is likely to be the contract or the payroll, with the latter being, perhaps, the only means whereby employees of the same company can affiliate themselves to each other. The basis for the 'psychological contract' (Robinson *et al.*, 1994), therefore, is not the formal bond with the employing organization. Instead it is the unwritten agreement that sets out mutual expectations between managers and employees. It is focused upon relations with immediate colleagues, the completion of particular time-specified and budgeted projects and the delivery of these according to certain 'professional' or 'quality' standards to clients or customers.

Such features are particularly apparent in some creative companies and these tend to be reinforced by the existence of occupational reference groups that encourage employees to orientate themselves towards extra-organizational criteria of performance. As a result, commitment to employing organizations can be diluted, with the psychological contract between employer and employee highly tenuous. Indeed, employees may develop orientations such that they perceive the employment relationship in a highly instrumental manner, first as a source for personal financial remuneration and, second, as a package of resources that can be 'exploited' for producing products and services that enhance their professional and occupational reputation.

Consequently, there are many organizational settings that are highly fragmented, with mechanisms of coordination often being implicit and ambiguously defined. Such organizational forms are in sharp contrast to those traditional bureaucratic paradigms that have tended to shape management thinking about 'preferred' and 'efficient' organizational processes. It is for this reason that many organizations are seen to lack leadership, direction or account-ability and that, to be more efficient, it is necessary to introduce hierarchically based, explicit control mechanisms.[4]

It is evident that in most creative organizations there will be an interplay between explicit, formal control mechanisms on the one hand, and informal, colleague-determined, implicit processes on the other. This is particularly the case where creativity is the basis upon which core, corporate work processes are organized. However, the tensions can sometimes be countered by, for example, marginalizing or outsourcing creative operations. As has been emphasized, creativity, as a social process, tolerates autonomy, nonconformity and indeterminacy. Informal and the tacitly understood work processes that do not require a formally imposed management structure will nearly always be present. However, to conclude that this must be the main aim of organizational structure would be to overlook the diversity of organizational forms that actually exist within the creative industries. The independent variation of the two axes of coordination and control creates diversity as organizations search for ways to resolve tensions as well as improve structures and strategies. Even within the same company, there will be work settings where such variations are felt more acutely than in others. Consequently, there will be diverse organizational outcomes associated with the extent to which processes are formalized and managed through alternative coordination and control mechanisms.

The following diagram offers a basis according to which such tensions are reflected in a diversity of work practices, operating procedures and control mechanisms (see Figure 4.1).

With *commercial bureaucracies*, the mechanisms of both control and coordination are highly explicit and formalized. The primary aim of these organizations is to exploit creativity for the purposes of making profit. There is an ongoing attempt by management to impose rules and regulations that govern the means whereby clearly defined goals are to be achieved. The outcome will be an emphasis on hierarchical reporting mechanisms according to which the performance of employees is monitored, measured and appraised. There will be a preference for clarity of roles and,

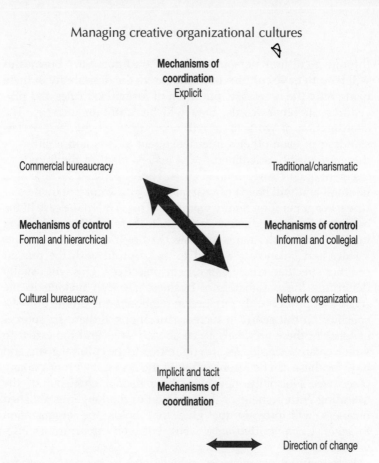

Figure 4.1 Types of creative organization: dimensions of coordination and control

therefore, a tendency to have precisely defined job descriptions. In view of the characteristics of creative work processes – based upon autonomy, nonconformity and indeterminacy – such organizations will be characterized by tension. The outcome will be ongoing negotiation about the legitimacy and necessity of explicit and formalized coordination and control mechanisms.

In the *traditional* or *charismatic* organization, by contrast, there is a high level of coordination through shared values and employee commitment to them but the mechanisms of formal control are relatively less developed. Their business aims are made explicit

99

through a cultural, personal or family tradition. Such businesses will tend to have cultures that emphasize the desirability of there being only the necessary minimum of formalized rules and procedures. In other words, they will be 'anti-bureaucratic'. The coordination of work tasks will occur through the tacit understanding of each other's interdependent talents and abilities as these are visibly orientated to the achievement of the founder's vision or other clearly defined goals. These businesses will tend to be small and will have been established by the current owners or by earlier generation family members. This is often the case in the book publishing industry. As a result, there is often a 'guiding mission' which stipulates the objectives of the business, ensures loyalty and balances the need to make profit with the pursuit of other specified creative or artistic objectives. This will usually determine the parameters of business decision making in the sense that profit is only pursued in relation to the production of a specific cultural genre. In such organizations, if there are sources of tension, these are likely to be about values and the extent to which creative employees are committed to the cultural goals, and how far these can be reconciled with the necessary profit-making objectives. Normally, however, the personal charisma of the founding entrepreneur or the tradition of the longer established business will provide the glue that holds the organization together. Uncommitted employees will seek opportunities elsewhere.

With *cultural bureaucracies*, which tend to be public service organizations, goals are usually diffuse because of the need to be publicly accountable for resources while at the same time achieving high cultural standards. There is, in other words, the need to be culturally effective but also publicly responsible. The outcome is organizational forms that are characterized by a high degree of formalized control, rather like the civil service but without similar formalized mechanisms of coordination. In these organizations, there will usually be clearly defined control processes consisting of hierarchically structured authority relations – 'referral upwards' being the traditional mechanism in the BBC (Kumar, 1975: 76). However, coordination of tasks and projects within the overall division of labour is achieved through subdivision into relatively autonomous departments, units and operational sectors.

It is in such organizations – by comparison with the other three types – that there is likely to be the greatest clash of cultures when they face increasing commercial pressures. It is inherent in the relations between those engaged in the management process on the one hand and creative employees responsible for the production and output of cultural products on the other. They are, therefore, characterized by a potentially high degree of tension which is usually resolved by attempts to 'ring-fence' the areas of autonomy, nonconformity and indeterminacy which are essential for the creative process. Bureaucratic organization, rules and procedures can serve this purpose. However, attempts to restrict the space within the fence – as witnessed by management changes at the BBC in the 1990s – are likely to generate considerable resentment among creative staff.

Network organizations lack mechanisms of explicit, formal control and of coordination. This is because they tend to be very small, consisting of either the independent providers of specialist talents, expertise or services or of networks made up of teams of such providers. Sometimes the latter may trade as registered companies or partnerships but, more likely than not, they will be self-employed or the employers of no more than three or four staff. What characterizes these businesses is the absence of a significant employment relationship and of organizational structures. They are, quite simply, too small to have either formalized control or coordinating mechanisms. When there are employees, relations between colleagues and with proprietors tend to be highly informal. The work process is undertaken on the basis of mutual adjustment with a tacit understanding of each other's duties, competences and responsibilities. Since such businesses allow a high degree of autonomy, nonconformity and indeterminacy – and this is their attraction for many creative employees – there are few internal tensions. Any tensions that do arise are likely to derive from external pressures which translate into tight time schedules, lack of resources, and the need to maintain network contacts. Such forms of organization are increasingly found in the television industry as a result of reregulation in the 1980s and the outsourcing of many activities previously undertaken in-house.

No single organization can be neatly fitted into one of the above quadrants. Since they are subject to continuous change, often driven by external as well as internal conflicting pressures, 'real' organizations rarely attain a stable state according to which operating procedures are clearly established on a longer term basis. Even so, the organizational characteristics of some creative companies are more likely to reflect these than others. This is particularly so in those where control mechanisms have been imposed such that the opportunities for the exercise of creativity – based upon autonomy, nonconformity and indeterminacy – are low. This is the case in commercial bureaucracies but not, by contrast, in network forms of organization where the fluidity of internal and external operating procedures is conducive to high levels of creativity in the absence of even weakly established mechanisms of control. With the latter, creativity is likely to be expressed in the continuous development of innovative products and services while the exercise of control is through market relations rather than by internal organizational processes.

While there have been some general changes affecting the structuring of creative organizations, these are leading to diametrically opposed outcomes. One the one hand, there is a tendency towards the *commercial bureaucracy* while, on the other, there are shifts towards the *network* model. In contrast, *traditional/charismatic* organizations and *cultural bureaucracies* are both in relative decline because of changes in ownership patterns and cultures in different creative sectors. In other words, these types of organization are being pulled in both directions simultaneously. The pattern of such changes is the subject of discussion in the next chapter.

Notes

1 For a discussion of this concept see, for example, Alvesson (1993) and Frost *et al.* (1991).
2 The network type of organization is, however, untypical in advertising. Networks would mean the fragmentation of the functions performed in a large agency, such as client relations, account management, art direction and copywriting. Some of these functions can be, and are in some cases, performed by freelancers and very small firms but there is a limit to how far this can go.

3 The two principles have a more than passing resemblance to the ideas of system integration (coordination) and social integration (control) found in social theory. The distinction was first articulated in the work of David Lockwood (1964) and it has been widely used in the study of large- and small-scale social systems.

4 In many countries, the 'reform' of professional organizations is associated with the implementation of such processes. It often generates conflict, as those with expert, specialist and technical knowledge resent the imposition of explicit control mechanisms upon work activities that were previously conducted with a considerable degree of autonomy.

5

TRENDS IN CREATIVE ORGANIZATIONS

The types of organization defined in the previous chapter point to some of the dynamic changes which have been taking place in the creative industries. The research data illustrate the nature of these changes in some detail. They show that there are strong tendencies among creative organizations to adopt new ways of organizing work processes and new types of coordination and control, in order to meet the demands of increasing competition, to take advantage of the opportunities created by new technologies, and to respond to changes in the business environment. These themes are now explored through the evidence from two major sectors of the creative industries: publishing and broadcasting.

Book publishing

The publishing sector most clearly illustrates the shift towards commercial bureaucracy and away from traditional forms. Traditionally, book publishing was characterized by a low level of ownership concentration. Many were attracted to publishing occupations by the idea of using their creative skills in writing, editing and criticism. Their personal ambitions were expressed through the mechanism of establishing their own business, either in the form of sole proprietorships or in the establishment of part-nerships. The history of the industry also includes many examples of editors, commissioning agents and those engaged in other specialist functions within large publishing companies who have set up their own businesses. Their motives were varied, ranging from a desire for personal autonomy, or the wish to publish ideo-logically, culturally or aesthetically distinctive products, through to the ambition to exploit a perceived niche in the market place for a specialist range of books. Such a tradition continues to persist and, indeed, is reinforced by developments in information tech-nology as well as by broader organizational changes in the pub-lishing industry. For instance, the continuing development of freelance and subcontracting relations for the book publishing process encourages such forms of cultural, as well as economic, entrepreneurship because the start-up costs are low. The only assets required are the intellectual, artistic and creative talents of the proprietors concerned, a minimum amount of capital outlay and, possibly, networks of personal contacts with authors.

However, a major reason attracting those with creative talents to set up their independent publishing houses has been the shift towards bureaucratization within the industry. A number of forces have contributed to this development. First, as described earlier, the amalgamation and merger of a large number of inde-pendent publishing businesses brought in its wake processes of corporate rationalization and the increasing salience of bureau-cratic principles. These tendencies continue as companies identify their core competences and sources of profit, and spin off their perceived peripheral publishing activities to others who, in turn, identify these as central to their business plans. Second, publish-ing firms have applied more strictly rational accounting practices. Traditionally, they operated on a break-even basis since the primary objective was to produce books as cultural products of a particular literary genre. The transfer in ownership of such busi-nesses has made profitability the prime goal with the published books perceived primarily as sources of earnings. Third, the growth of a mass market and development of mass marketing techniques for blockbusters and best-sellers enables publishers to produce extended runs of a very limited range of titles. In such businesses, with the exception of the creative act of writing (and even this can be highly routinized through 'formatted' and 'ghost writing' methodologies), there is extensive application of clearly defined, routine-governed control mechanisms that dictate the work process, from commissioning to production, distribution and sales. Both in-house and out-of-house relationships associated with these activities are conditioned by the rigorous application of cost accounting practices.

To the extent that commercial bureaucratic and the contrasting but complementary network forms of organization are becoming increasingly dominant within the publishing sector, cultural bureaucratic and traditional/charismatic forms are in decline. There is a tendency for large-scale publishing organizations to prioritize managerial over creative functions. They are either following the strategy of segregation described in Chapter 3, where creative tasks are outsourced by using the talents of freelance editors, graphic designers and sub-editors, or, if these tasks are retained in-house, the strategy of incorporation. In the latter case, they consist of a small core of experts who subscribe to the superordinate management values of efficiency, cost-effectiveness and profit-and-loss. In this sense, their creative values are incorporated within – and often subordinated to – management objectives. Equally, traditional/charismatic forms of organization are in decline as a result of cultural shifts that have occurred within publishing. Traditionally, these have been either family-owned houses or businesses set up by those who wish to escape from the commercially driven control mechanisms of larger publishing companies. Either way, relationships within such businesses tend to be highly particularistic and informal, located as they are within essentially small-scale operations. Staff recruitment tends, therefore, to incorporate personal, as well as creative, expertise. The organization places a strong emphasis upon commitment to books as contributions to culture (as distinct from sources of profit) and to the business as expressed by personal loyalty to senior colleagues and to the traditions of the house.

The interview data illustrate many of these contrasting forms of organization as found within the publishing industry. The pronounced commercial ideology of such businesses is reflected in the following description given by the senior editorial director of a major publishing company:

Well, on the paperback side the economies of scale now in paperback publishing mean that one can print 12,500–15,000 copies to begin with and then reprint steadily. It isn't a question of you have to print 100,000 to make an economy, because after about 15,000–20,000 copies you're not getting any benefit from that, in fact you're having a high cash lock-up ... Even with a new title where we are expecting to get 150,000 out on subscription, we'll print that in sort of 50,000 bites and we'll send 50,000 off to Australia, we'll supply some of the major wholesalers, and by publication date we might well have done three or four printings.

This is the language of commercial efficiency, quantifiable measures and returns on investment. However, there is also an appreciation of the organizational implications of different genres. For example, the publishing director of the children's division of an international conglomerate describes the contrasting commercial logic of books either for children or adults:

If one was sitting here wanting short-term profits one would have closed children's publishing years ago. The sales pattern of children's books is different in the sense that adult books are bought expensively, promoted expensively and sold very quickly, so that on publication day you're expecting to get out into the bookshops 80 per cent of what you're going to sell. Children's books have quite a different pattern in that what we call subscription figure, the book sales on the first publication are often pathetic because there isn't space, there isn't the hype attached to children's books. But what you're more likely to get is a much steadier pattern over a longer period of time when a book is being tested by teachers, widely discussed and assimilated and found to be a success with children and then it gets into the core curriculum, the core range of books that schools will like and accept and use. So the whole pattern is different when one is doing one's financial appraisal, one is doing it on a much longer term basis, not quick money out, quick money up front, it's a long steady pattern which in the end is a different kind of business to buying a blockbuster adult novel which is all going to be out in the first three months. If you haven't sold it in the first three months, well, it's returns from here on in. The returns rate is a different level of business, and that's got to be borne in mind.

The picture that emerges of the typical commercial bureaucracy is one in which the high volume of sales dictates the work process and, particularly, the selection of creative works that are chosen as publishable titles. This is evident later during the interview when the same publishing director states:

The way initially is by individual editors having a feeling and discussing it with other individual editors and we do have a weekly meeting at which most things are discussed, although a meeting of ten people isn't necessarily going to be the best judge. Frequently one just knows that something is absolutely terrific. *One knows it is not just because of the item itself, the project itself, but also from the way we can publish, and that is to do with past history, where we sell best, what we can and can't cope with, what our production department can and can't cope with.* (Our italics)

Hence, there are severe constraints against risk taking or developing new ideas unless it can be incorporated within a particular production format. This is reinforced by the market context within which large publishers are compelled to operate. For this particular editorial director, competition for shelf space in multiple bookshops was a key factor determining commissioning policy:

The difficulty there is that they have a limit in their stores of, I think, at the moment it's no more than 24 per cent of their shelving will be given over to books, so however big or small the shop is, that's the limit. And, yes, they will occasionally try new books to put into their range but unfortunately the danger is that when they try a new book they have to take out an old book and you have to hope it's somebody else's old book they're taking out not one of ours, and they do it all by testing. They will trial a book in x many shops and if it doesn't sell y hundred copies in the first week or the second week, then that's gone, and so it is a very sort of stern testing. So there are different customers with different needs and

I in my role as publisher . . . I'm not just an editorial person, *I have to be aware of all those things and I have to pass that on to all my editors as well, that we have to be aware of all these constraints. And it's no good sitting in an ivory tower saying 'But this is brilliant' if we can't reach the market.* (Our italics)

These comments reflect the increasing probability that commercial pressures will dictate the internal decision-making processes of publishing companies. Equally, these observations reflect the degree to which such businesses are reluctant to innovate with new products and to nurture creativity, as distinct from conformity, within their operating processes. The general direction of change in the publishing industry is neatly summarized in the following comment by a well-known and highly regarded figure in the industry:

Well, I come from a sort of background where I've experienced every kind of operation. Because, to begin with, [the original publishing house] was a rather old-fashioned, autocratic . . . run by the man who founded it. He then sold it to [a media conglomerate] and they had a rather hands-off approach to their belongings. In other words, they left well alone, as long as one came up to expectations. Then they sold to [a major international publisher] who took a different line. They took an exceedingly hands-on line and were much in favour of amalgamation, coordination. They were quite obsessed with structure and charts showing who reported to who, and who was at the end of which dotted line. So I suppose I've experienced all three kinds of approach and I found that the last one was, not surprisingly, the least attractive because it seemed to me to squash the creativity of the publishing company. *Because I think a publishing company flourishes best if the contacts between the publishing company and the authors are at the core of the operation.* And if you become totally taken up with a series of meetings and inter-relationships between departments you don't actually have very much time to devote to authors. The authors then get extremely cross because they lead lonely lives, and they begin to get upset and drift away to someone else. (Our italics)

This speaker identifies the core of the creative process with the role of the editors, whether they are operating in the context of a large or a small organization. The stages of his career express a commitment to this idea:

> I think that the editorial aspect of publishing is the most important. It's not the only one, of course; there's marketing, production, and all the other aspects of publishing, but if you don't have books and authors you can't actually start publishing at all and I found that my own editorial basis was being eroded and one of the reasons for this, in a big corporation, I think, was that inevitably if one big corporate company buys a series of smaller companies, it wants to integrate them.

His own preferences are clear. Only the smaller type of organization of which he is currently managing director can provide the autonomy which he feels is necessary. This recently established company has many of the features of the traditional/charismatic form of organization which, although no longer the dominant form, continues as a significant category of business within publishing.

A number of features help to account for the relative decline but two are particularly significant. First, there are the biographical experiences of people like the respondent just quoted who, having developed their personal expertise within relatively small publishing houses find themselves – through corporate takeovers – as employees within tightly controlled, commercial, bureaucratically structured organizations. They then opt out of such structures by setting up their own small businesses so that they can recreate the traditional/charismatic forms of organization with which they are personally familiar. Second, such businesses, irrespective of how they are established, tend to be set up by those who particularly resent control relationships unless, of course, they themselves are exercising the control. This, together with a desire to establish creative work processes – that is, those which nurture autonomy, indeterminacy and nonconformity – leads to a heavy reliance upon informal working relations. Paradoxically, however, these will be organized around the founder–owner(s) and their personal view of the creative process, which sets out well-defined parameters of what should and should not be published. This fosters employee dependency and inhibits the development of new, alternative creative processes. The contradictory nature of these smaller organizations is reflected in observations by the same respondent, who described his business in the following terms:

> Well, the structure is in a sense both tight because it's small, and loose because it's fairly unregimented. I mean, we don't have to have, as probably you do if you are in a large corporation, a set of interlocking groups because it is easy in a small environment, as this office is, for everyone to talk the whole time. So we don't have a lot of meetings. We have one editorial meeting which covers a lot of other things per week, and we have a board meeting once a month and that's it, otherwise we just do it on a day-to-day basis.

There may be little evidence of formal structure in such organizations – a feature that is often emphasized with pride by such proprietors – but the control mechanisms are expressed through other means. Instead of clearly defined procedures stipulating duties and responsibilities, there are tightly knit interpersonal relations and strongly pronounced preferences and expectations about taste, standards, what the market will and will not accept. They constitute a strong organizational culture in which employees are obliged to participate. Consequently, through a process of selective recruitment, socialization and charismatic influence, the specific meaning of creativity is established and maintained. Noncompliance by employees constitutes incompatibility or a personality clash for which there is no place, in the longer term, in the smaller publishing company.

In one of the larger firms in the category of small publishers, a similar pattern was evident. The managing director was aware of the extent to which business growth could lead to the emergence of a large organization that would then require structures and control mechanisms which he was keen to avoid. Instead, he preferred to manage through informal relationships and a cohesive culture emphasizing company loyalty and conformity. As he stated:

> Well, its very interesting this. I mean, there is a weekly meeting, but I actually don't think the major decisions are taken

in the meeting. They're supposed to be, but there's a lot of trading outside of that; as in my case, making decisions autonomously. It's a tricky question. It's got an awful lot to do with personalities . . . On the whole, we all know what types of book, loosely speaking, we try to acquire. But I think the answer to your question, really, is that it's not very formal although it can be dressed up to look as though it is. I think the weekly meeting has a function; it distributes information – but people also air their views on books they're thinking of taking on. *There's about ten or twelve people at the meeting and if it's generally thought the book I'm taking on isn't worth taking on, it doesn't necessarily mean I don't. You can sit there and think, 'Well they don't know as much about this as I do'.* (Our italics)

His personal influence remains strong and is a main source of job satisfaction.

It is clear from these brief observations that there is a diversity of management practices within the publishing industry. The tendency is towards the domain of large commercial bureaucracies within the industry but, alongside this, there is the ongoing evolution of smaller, entrepreneurial forms that are structured according to traditional/charismatic principles. Although the latter often exhibit an appearance of creativity, this may lack empirical substance. At best, any organizational creativity – in the form of autonomous, indeterminate and nonconformist work practices – is tightly constrained by 'dominant personalities' who, as managing directors, founding managers or founder–editors, impose their opinions about preferred cultural products upon their junior colleagues, as well as stipulating 'informally' how tasks should be undertaken. They often display the characteristics of 'charismatic authority' which Max Weber describes as an alternative to the legal–rational forms found in a bureaucracy (Weber, 1978: 241). Close-knit interpersonal relations, face-to-face negotiation and the selection of staff according to criteria that emphasize acceptability and compatibility as well as personal competence sustain a compliant culture that channels creativity in specific directions. It limits creative independence in a wider sense. It is often for this reason that those who have had experience of working in a small business consider resigning in order to set up their own publishing enterprise. Their own identification of a niche in the market for a particular genre or type of output, together with the search for personal creative expression, leads them to set up businesses within which the creativity of others is inhibited. Such is the contradiction of traditional/charismatic small firms. It helps to account for many of the career experiences of those who move within the publishing industry; moving from large commercial bureaucratic companies, in the first instance, and then shifting between various small firms.

Traditional/charismatic forms of publishing organization, including their modern variants, are in decline not simply because of the dominance of commercial bureaucracies through mergers and acquisitions but also as a result of developments in publishing and printing technologies. The phenomenon of desktop publishing has brought virtually all aspects of production within range of the small-scale specialist organization using computing and information technologies. Undoubtedly, there is a continuing niche for both general and specialist small publishers but the interdependency of small technology-based organizations represents a distinctive alternative. We refer to the myriad desktop publishers as network organizations simply because they are highly dependent upon personal networks for their economic survival. Also, they are typically one-person businesses, utilizing advances in information technology to produce books, periodicals or internet services which are then sold to purchasers through direct advertising and mail order. Network organizations, however, are now probably more pronounced within the television industry than in publishing. It is to this sector that we now turn in order to illustrate further the diversity of management practices in the creative industries; namely, the features of cultural bureaucracies as well as of network organizations.

Television broadcasting

Within the television sector, cultural bureaucracy characterizes those organizations in which there are clearly defined management processes which involve the segregation of those engaged in administration from those engaged directly in the creative process. Accordingly, there is often an acute awareness of a distinction between 'them' – management – and 'us', that is, those who actually produce and deliver the cultural output. Traditionally, the BBC was the major institution representing this form of organization but the regional television companies in the ITV sector had similar features on account of the system of public regulation and supervision. During the 1990s, the cultural bureaucratic form has been in decline in both the public and commercial sectors of television broadcasting. The Broadcasting Act of 1990 marked a significant shift towards a more commercial and competition-orientated system. It articulated a number of themes including the need to encourage competition and offer greater choice to consumers. At the same time, it endorsed the role of public service institutions in the broadcasting system and the continuing need for regulation. This translated in practice into policies for the reduction of overheads and other costs, independent production quotas, and policies such as Producer Choice to encourage internal competition[1]. It encouraged the further separation between the traditional television functions of production and broadcasting which began with Channel 4. The growth of small specialized independent television programme production companies has fostered the development of network forms of organization, while their larger counterparts have adopted commercial bureaucratic types of organizational structure. This is particularly evident in the changes occurring within the BBC and the larger, publicly owned, profit-orientated television companies. Even so, the changes at the BBC are far from complete and the interviews undertaken during the present research indicate only partially resolved conflicts between those who wished to impose commercial bureaucratic methodologies upon an organization and those more accustomed to cultural bureaucratic forms. Accordingly, new divisions are tending to replace those that, in the past, led to organizational barriers between those responsible for the management and administration of the organization as a whole and others who were delegated to manufacture and broadcast programmes. Our analysis shows that, empirically, it is often misleading to designate an objective, commonly agreed boundary but, in practice, this is how perceptions of organizational processes are often perceived. This is forcefully

expressed by a respondent from a drama department in independent television:

> The nature of the management here is really that we are a link
> between a very formal bureaucratic structure which sched-
> ules and generates revenue by selling advertising and then
> reallocates revenue to make programmes. And we're the link
> with the outside world which is the creative link – writers,
> producers and directors – and it's really liaising between
> those two bodies. Fundamentally, it's linking those two
> worlds which are fundamentally unsympathetic by nature
> but have to be made to work through that [structure] because
> the individuals on the outside – the talent: writers, actors,
> producers, directors – will work on their individual careers
> and their individual agendas which are entirely unrelated to
> any formal structures such as promotion or whatever.

In the traditional hierarchy of large broadcasting organizations,
those involved in production are very aware of the dangers of
remote decision making about resources. This anecdote from a
senior manager in the BBC highlights the point:

> It worries me that decisions are being made by people who
> haven't the faintest idea of the implications of some of the
> decisions they make. We try and take senior management
> staff out on location, and I remember I took a general man-
> ager out on location. Now, he was a general manager of a very
> big area . . . , responsible for a great deal of people's lives,
> money, decisions, and his staff worked on location mainly.
> We went to a location . . . and when we drove over the hill in
> his car, there was the circus there (they call it the circus
> because of the cars, and there's the banging all over the place
> and there's the portaloos and the generator and the sparks'
> van and everything was there) and he said: 'Good God,
> there's a fair there.' I said: 'That fair is your production.' He
> said: 'What do you mean, what is this?' And there were 147
> people on location and I said to him – he didn't believe it, he
> thought I was pulling his leg – and we drove all the way
> down and I said: 'Let me walk you round', and he said: 'Good
> God, what can all this be costing?' I said: 'For Christ's sake,

have you never been on location before ?' And he'd been in the job six years, running people who work on location, and he'd never been on location.

There is, of course a large overlap between the 'two worlds' of managerial and creative activities – a fact which is recognized in the following remarks by a manager responsible for factual programming in a regional television company:

> Most producers would hate to be called 'managers'. Managers, management is quite a dirty word in television throughout, because they're the people who stop things and say 'No' all the time – which is not necessarily true, but that's the impression producers have. But, in fact, they are [managers] because they have to motivate, they have to manage their teams, they have to have a degree of responsibility over the money.

The distinction which applies is between aspects of *coordination* (the aims, objectives and limits imposed by controllers, executives and business managers) and *control* (the organization of the work process by editors, producers and directors). Cultural bureaucracy is a form of organization which stresses the separation between these two spheres of activity.

If the cultural bureaucracy within television reflects a divide between managers and those engaged in the creative process, it also expresses the need to extend a considerable degree of operational autonomy to those engaged in the latter. In other words, a formalized management bureaucracy 'oversees' a work process which possesses a number of key features. First, it is often highly structured on the basis of time schedules and deadlines; programme projects have to be sequenced in order to coordinate a large inventory of talents and skills that are required to produce the final product. Second, there often remain areas of uncertainty that interrupt this scheduling process and thereby constitute management 'problems'. These, in the drama departments of television organizations, can range from the volatility of artists' temperaments to inappropriate weather conditions or obtaining access to physical locations. But third, and possibly most important of all, the creative process is structured on the basis of mutual adjustment whereby individual effort is coordinated within teams. Although these are highly structured in terms of scheduling and allocation of duties, they are, nevertheless, self-managing in the sense that, in order for them to complete their tasks, it is necessary for management to delegate operational responsibilities to them. This contributes to a culture and practices in which aesthetic criteria are important but the autonomy of creative employees is qualified by the constraints of budgets, output indicators and operational deadlines. Many of these issues – which, in themselves, constitute spheres of managerial uncertainty – are reflected in the following observations from the producer of a major BBC drama series:

> Once you've got the go-ahead, you've commissioned the script, you get the script, you employ a director and then assemble what you hope is a good team. Hopefully they all work together. This doesn't always work out. You can get a complete clash of personalities; that's always the worry. The main thing you're up against with filming is weather and the schedule. There's never long enough. There's no ideal schedule. You're always trying to do something in a very short time . . . I think the skill is picking the right mix of people in order that the thing runs efficiently. Partly through having worked for such a long time, I know an awful lot of people. It's knowing the people, their work and their temperament, which I do. How would I achieve it if I came in totally fresh – I suppose you'd have to spend all your time talking to people and interviewing them . . . you can't just assess it on their work, the personality is very important. Often, people don't understand this.

This comment illustrates the extent to which media and creative organizations are often seen to be non-meritocratic in their selection processes and to operate on the basis of closed or exclusive personal networks which outsiders have difficulty in penetrating. Alongside technical and artistic ability, the composition of work teams is made up of those who see themselves as personally compatible with each other and, hence, friendship and 'who you know' can be important criteria in setting up these teams. Equally, however, these same features reinforce the openness and flexibility of television companies in that those recruited as personal assistants, secretaries and lower grade administrators can find themselves allocated production duties, thereby enabling them to become part of the creative team and, accordingly, to nurture longer term career strategies. Certainly, these processes enable media businesses to portray themselves as open organizations within which talent, creativity and, often, ill-defined subjective attributes are recognized and rewarded. To manage such processes requires skills in team management, especially in order to coordinate the activities of a diverse range of people within the constraints of tight time schedules and financial budgets. The director of a well known BBC drama serial commented:

> I think one of the main jobs as director is you have to get the best out of everybody ... you have to facilitate their area of expertise so that jointly it becomes more than the sum of its parts. And that's obviously part of management: motivating people, making sure that everybody's going for the same thing. Because, very often, people are all trying to make a different film which is hopeless ... You have to have the film running in your head the whole time so that you know how it's going to work. But, you have to be able to communicate that to other people and a lot of people break down in not being able to explain what their vision is of a particular film to everyone who's working with it because people can't get inside your mind. So it's all very well having a very good film running in your head but you have to be able to make it real for other people and they have to be able to make it possible.

This, of course, requires collaborative team working and group dynamics based as much upon personal compatibility as technical and creative competence. An assistant floor manager working for a different drama series observes that

> You work together so closely, you see people very early in the morning when they're tired and they're hung-over and they're at their worst, perhaps, and you see them late at night when you've had a meal and you've been together all day working, eating, drinking, whatever ... So you know a lot about people in a very short amount of time. Quite often

it's about work, you know more about how they work rather than them personally, but you get a very, very intense relationship I suppose.

The pattern of work in drama production is one of high intensity and long working hours, but with periods of relaxation within work. These informal episodes also reinforce the dynamics of team working:

> We all work together. Everybody helps each other and, if one person or one group of people is fed up and they're not feeling like they want to be helpful, that makes life difficult. We're here a long time. I mean, we're here for twelve hours, that's one and a half normal working days, that's a long time. You have to enjoy it. And you enjoy it by being pleasant and sort of socializing with the people you're with. You have to behave as if tea breaks are like being in the pub with somebody. That you actually enjoy doing this because, if it is was all a drag, it would be awful.

Cultural bureaucracies, then, are characterized by *both* formalized management structures *and* loosely coupled informal working relationships. It is the latter that constitute the organizing principles according to which the relevant media products are manufactured and, as such, cultural bureaucracies are generally characterized by a divide that separates the creative process from the formalized management function. Each of these spheres of activity is separated in terms of attributes, interpersonal relations, dress codes, working practices, norms and organizational values. These differences prevent the imposition of integrated and unitary organizational cultures. Consequently, issues of management control and employee compliance are consistently regarded as problematic. This is reinforced by the existence of an external labour market wherein those engaged in the creative process can be highly mobile, shifting from one employer to the next, as well as being able to sell their services as freelancers. Hence, in the cultural bureaucracy, the organizational commitment of creative and technical employees is typically problematic. It tends to be managed on the basis of personal loyalties with colleagues who are engaged upon the same production project. Thus, the length of

projects and the nature of the interpersonal relations in conjunction with these will often determine whether or not employee
commitment to a particular employer extends from the short term
into the longer term.

The problem of commitment and accountability partly accounts
for management attempts to change the nature of organizations
operating as cultural bureaucracies, to make them operate in ways
resembling their commercial counterparts. It is this that constitutes the new managerialism at the BBC and, essentially, it represents a partial attempt to *incorporate* creative processes. It
endeavours to curtail operational autonomy and to impose tighter
constraints and greater accountability upon those responsible for
the production of programmes as well as other managers. As a
result, the traditional divide between management and creative
workers becomes eroded as the latter are compelled to adopt
working practices and to manufacture products by adopting cultures and structures similar to those found in any large-scale
manufacturing organization. Costs drive production and the
creative process becomes routinized and financially accountable
in television organizations in a manner similar to that of large
publishing companies. A BBC manager describes the meetings
which embody the commercialized form of control:

> I have a variety of routine meetings . . . On a weekly basis I
> have a routine meeting of my administrative team which
> includes my deputy manager, my finance assistant, the
> administrative assistant, the management assistant and my
> secretary . . . We have a monthly personnel routine meeting
> . . . and then we have a quarterly group personnel meeting.
> We have a biweekly publicity meeting where we have a brief-
> ing with our PR man . . . We have a weekly meeting with the
> head of department. We have a monthly meeting with all the
> departmental managers, and a quarterly meeting with the
> production associates, a monthly meeting with the producers
> and the directors . . . I think the problem that we have here is
> that the corporation is going to go into a pseudo-commercial
> world. We're trying to run like the outside world but actually
> what we do is have a lot of the constraints of a bureaucracy.

Equally, the independent television companies, in a similar way to the BBC, have imposed more cost-conscious and profit-orientated organizational structures:

> What the company has done is to hive off its major departmental functions into separate cost-centred functions. Some are separate companies, some are part of a group but they are all separately managed divisions with their own profit centres.

Those who were trained within cultural bureaucracies where programme making and money management were strictly separate activities are often very conscious of the shift to a more commercial orientation:

> Well, it's a bit odd because [the company] is making a packet selling advertising space. It then effectively allocates a percentage of its income to making programmes. What it is now demanding, at the same time, is that people who are making those programmes *also make a profit* ... It's a strange bit of management, I think. (Our italics)

Once the supply of programmes or service is organized through cost or profit centres, employees may compare the advantages and disadvantages of conducting similar activities in an independent form of organization.

With the increasing emphasis upon costs and profits, the evolution of the commercial bureaucracy in the television industry – like book publishing – has thus brought in its wake the growth of network organizations. These tend to be relatively small in size, having been established by those with considerable experience of particular aspects of television production. These 'independent' companies are inclined to specialize in the production of particular genres, either in response to commissions from the BBC, the ITV network or Channel 4, or for sale to broadcasting organizations in the international market place. Some specialize in documentaries, others in drama and light entertainment, others in natural history or news. The growth of these smaller network organizations is a further stage in the segregation between the production and broadcasting functions that were once combined within the single organization, either the BBC or the traditional regional television companies. Legislation and management

121

strategies created separate markets for the supply and purchase of programming, as well as for a variety of specialized production services. The outcome has been the fragmentation of this market into a variety of niches for which smaller independent companies provide specialist programming and technical services. In this increasingly competitive and differentiated market, it is necessary for companies to operate on very low overhead costs. Accordingly, such businesses operate on the basis of networks, whereby a small core of relatively permanent staff hire other specialists on short-term, fixed-time contracts. These freelancers are highly mobile between one network organization and the next, depending on the demand for their labour in relation to a sequence of one-off projects. Thus, the television industry as a whole is becoming characterized by growing numbers of freelancers and other self-employed subcontractors who offer their services, not only to smaller independent companies but also to the BBC and its major competitors, as the cost-driven imperatives of the commercial bureaucracy supersede those of the creative and publicly orientated cultural bureaucracy.

Elements of the network form of organization, therefore, are becoming increasingly apparent alongside as well as within these larger operations. Producer Choice at the BBC, for example, is a manifestation of this. However, despite the increasing use of subcontractors and the hiring of freelancers on a short-term basis in large creative organizations, the pattern is particularly pronounced among small television production companies. According to the managing director of a small company specializing in factual programmes,

> You have to keep core staff down to the absolute minimum and, if you've got people permanently on the books, then they've got to have editorial skills, production skills and management skills, and they're very rare birds at the moment. Perhaps they won't be in another ten years' time. But you have to keep them down otherwise you go under because the overheads are too high . . . You should really have about, let's say, around three people who are effectively producer–managers and you will probably have a back-up staff of as many people immediately needed to help them –

that's business manager, production manager, accountant – and that's it really. You've got to keep it down to that minimum. *Then you hire people on as you get projects and they come in when the project's switched on and go when the project's switched off.* Then you try not to have them go, so you have limited powers to retain people by just organizing things so that one project is succeeded by another. (Our italics)

To a limited extent, these small network forms of organization take on the characteristics of traditional/charismatic types of business found in the publishing industry. The tendencies are less acute than in publishing because of the very different cultural legacy of television as a flow medium broadcasting to mass audiences but, as in publishing, businesses can operate around the talents, reputation and charisma of the founder or owner–director. As a result, a well-pronounced organizational culture can be formed which can have a significant impact upon business strategies. It can, for example, determine the staff recruitment process and lead to a reluctance to use temporary freelancers on the grounds that their commitment to the values of the business will, inevitably, be limited. Further, it can be a constraint upon business growth, since founder–owners may only wish to produce a fixed volume of programmes of a particular genre and with a scale of operation which they feel personally capable of managing. Finally, a strictly imposed set of beliefs about working practices and what the business should produce in the way of programmes can stand in the way of growth through acquisitions or merger with another company. If it occurs, growth is more likely to be organic. As one chief executive founder–owner stated:

I think that this company is about the right size now, to be able to cope with most of what it's likely to get by way of fuel [business] to keep it going . . . Acquisition doesn't work. It works for a bit but you read your . . . you read the rules on this industry, which is an ideas-based industry, and you find if ideas clashed – I mean, lots of things can clash . . . but if ideas clash you get real problems. If I was to say now, 'I want to double the size of this company and I'll do a deal with somebody who makes sports programmes', within weeks you'd find there'd be such a clash of cultures, it wouldn't work.

123

As with traditional/charismatic organizations in general, the future direction of this particular television company is shaped by the views of the founder and owner who, as chief executive, is able to dictate business strategy. This also shapes the nature of working relationships which, in both these and network forms of organization, tend to be highly informal. But there are differences in that, in the traditional/charismatic company, employees' commitment to management (for the reasons discussed earlier) can be more or less taken for granted. This is less likely to be the case in small network organizations in the television industry. Consequently, the management core, which incorporates the dimensions of both coordination and control, constantly has to negotiate working relations with both staff and freelancers hired on a short-term basis, since they operate in an industry which has an active labour market and where extensive personal contacts transcend organizational boundaries. The negotiated orders within network organizations can, therefore, incorporate a diversity of issues such as pay and working conditions through to the nature of interpersonal relations, the composition of work groups and decision-making processes. Thus, the organization and execution of tasks according to the principles of mutual adjustment reinforces the informality which is characteristic of network organizations within the television industry. Because these features are intrinsic to organizational creativity, they may be found anywhere in the network process which, in any case, tends to be weakly defined by comparison with the commercial or cultural bureaucratic forms. As far as those within the management core are concerned, informality may find the following expression. The chief executive of an independent production company describes the typical pattern of meetings as one which allows for lateral communication, informality and flexibility:

> The formal meetings that happen are very few. There's internal departmental meetings which are specific to the skills of the people who are having them. There will be a regular weekly development meeting just purely for all those who are concerned with development and those who will deal with the products of that development, to know what is happening . . . There's the business affairs group which attempts

to bring all the departments on a Tuesday morning to run through everything that we're doing, so that everyone in those departments – one person from the department, it doesn't have to be the head of that department – knows what is happening and has the duty of passing this back to everyone else in their department. Then there's a whole company meeting once every three months to take whatever questions are hot at the time. But it's a small place, and we're all in one building and it's all individually close . . . I don't think there's much status standing here. I think it's fairly open.

As another executive of a small television production company stated:

What [this business] does demand is the complete lack of hierarchy . . . I don't need to go around and impose upon them my view of how these things should be done; they come to me and say, 'I want to do it this way.' Providing it isn't a waste of money, I let them do it that way . . . We have a very long, I believe almost unique, reputation of not over-spending on our programmes or our clients, the television or anybody else, and that's due to the self-discipline of the individuals, it's not due to me . . . The budget is available to anyone who wants to see it.

The lack of hierarchy is closely linked with flexibility in work processes and relations. The speaker adopts a metaphor from film-making to convey the sense of this:

Management is a series of light and dark bits – it's not all light or all dark like . . . it's not draconian, it's flexible. It's hues and shades, it's not all black or all white. There are lots of subtleties involved and because there are people each person brings their own spectrum of subtleties and it's very important that the company should use those subtleties to the best of its advantage. Now most people say, can you speak a foreign language, or can you type, you know, those basic learnt skills. I'm not talking about those, I'm talking about things which are deep-rooted in people, that they want to do certain things . . . This company is a monument to people, to the way people like to do things, and that's the way I want it to be, and if it

125

fails, it fails smiling. It's not going to be one of those dark, gloomy things where there is an absentee manager, and nobody knows where the money goes, etc. This company is going to reflect the people within it, and that's what I want it to be like, and that's what our clients like. When they come here, they are amazed at the enthusiasm of the people.

Indeterminacy, which is an inevitable feature of this type of organization, is controlled by the personal influence of the chief executive. Interestingly, he uses a military analogy to explain 'control' and the contrasting image of children's games to describe 'creativity'.

I walk around, I spend my entire time walking around, I know everyone by their first names . . . Leading by example is what it's about. The classic management system is the army. The army is often used as a derogatory metaphor but if you take the US army, which is on the platoon system or what is known as the 'buddy' system where everybody feels responsible for anyone else. And the only hierarchy is that you know the person in charge will become the person in charge if there's a crisis. But up until that point, everybody's the same . . . If there's a crisis, I will run ahead and deal with that, I will manage it.

I still think I'm about 12 that's the trouble, and everybody's here to behave like a 12-year-old. *And I think one of the great things children have is the ability to organize games and actually business is a game . . . Children will do it by going into a corner huddled together, whispering, then coming out, telling the others what the rules are and then getting on with it. And I think that's the way you do it.* (Our italics)

Conclusion

It is, then, evident that there is a diversity of organizational forms within the creative industries. This is hardly surprising, given the variety of products, technologies, skills and markets that characterize them. Equally, differences in patterns of ownership, management traditions, size and degrees of public accountability shape the design of organizations. Notwithstanding these factors, however, the object of this chapter has been to demonstrate how the management process typically involves negotiated orders that shape the prevailing characteristics of creative organizations. In some circumstances formalized management processes have incorporated the creative processes – as in commercial bureaucratic forms of organization – such that the traditional divide between management and creativity (as found in cultural bureaucracies) no longer prevails. Indeed, the former is rapidly superseding the latter as publishing, television and other sectors of the creative industries find themselves increasingly in competition with each other in regional, national and international markets. At the same time, new manifestations of network organization have been developing, with creative processes which take the form of highly concentrated sources of energy organized in clusters. Their capacity for innovation is the key trading asset of such businesses. Without the continuous nurturing of creativity, there is little product innovation, resulting in ultimate business decline. In these organizations, formalized control mechanisms are minimal. However, the processes of mutual adjustment are linked with highly pronounced cultures which dictate, albeit informally, what is to be achieved and by what means. Traditional/charismatic forms of organization are equally structured according to informal practices but, in contrast with network organizations, their hierarchically imposed cultures, emanating from founders or owners (or their successors), demand employee compliance and, thereby, inhibit the personal autonomy, indeterminacy of outcomes, and nonconformity which are intrinsic to creativity. Although these forms of organization are continually reproduced, particularly as a result of business start-ups and various entrepreneurial ventures in different sectors of the creative industries, they probably represent an organizational dynamic that is in decline. It is, then, the commercial bureaucracy and the network organization that will, increasingly, constitute the paradigms according to which creative organizations will be structured in the years ahead.

127

Note

1 Producer Choice was a BBC scheme introduced in 1993 to promote a market in production facilities and services. Instead of being required to use in-house facilities, producers could choose to allocate their budgets freely between internal and external providers.

6

CREATIVE EMPLOYEES:
THEIR ATTITUDES AND VALUES

In this chapter, the analysis is extended to consider in somewhat more detail the characteristics of creative organizations, focusing particularly upon commercial bureaucracies and networks in the light of broader trends in technological change, governmental regulation and global competitive processes. Although commercial bureaucracies and network organizations may appear as opposites – an inference that may be drawn from Figure 4.1 on page 99 – the two are closely interrelated. The same developments that are bringing about commercial bureaucracies are also leading to networks operating as the external providers of various products and services.

Commercial bureaucracy: the psychological contract

Commercial bureaucracies are characterized by many of the traditional features of organization as expounded by such classical theorists as Max Weber and F. W. Taylor. The growth of such organizational forms within the creative industries was associated with managerial attempts to impose work practices according to a number of classical bureaucratic principles. However, in the

1990s, and sometimes earlier, many of these underlying principles have been challenged, with the result that the features of commercial bureaucracies are now somewhat different to those of earlier decades. Indeed, it is possible to distinguish between 'traditional' and 'new' forms of commercial bureaucracy, in terms of a number of organizational processes. Therefore, while a key process within some creative sectors has been the change towards commercial bureaucracy, this form of organization is, itself, undergoing fundamental transformation.

In itself, the imposition of the commercial bureaucratic form of organization in the creative industries led to the implementation of a number of core principles. First, there were attempts to rationalize the work activities of creative employees by encouraging the specialization of work tasks. In the 1960s and 1970s, the growth of large-scale creative organizations – drawing on legacies of the printing industry – motivated both management and trade unions to establish clearly defined job descriptions, occupational categories and performance-related reward systems. There were attempts in the television industry, particularly with the advent of the ITV regional companies, to curtail the autonomy and indeterminacy of employees by stipulating job duties, delineating specific spheres of responsibility and accountability, and establishing clearly defined line management reporting mechanisms. Clearer delineation of work roles was seen as a prerequisite for equitable payment systems and a counterbalance to the 'restrictive practices' of craft occupations. There were similar attempts in all the creative industries to impose managerial solutions which until the 1980s were considered to be symptomatic of efficient organization and good trade union practices. Evidence of the trend towards commercial bureaucracy could be found in the formalized processes whereby creative employees were subject to specified procedures, measurable performance indicators, and formal control mechanisms that would curtail their personal autonomy and indeterminacy and which, at the same time, would enforce their conformity to, and compliance with, organizational processes. In short, the aim was to bureaucratize creativity; that is, to impose control mechanisms upon personal initiative in order to incorporate creativity within a set of organizational rules.

Since it is necessary for these routines to be explicitly managed, instead of tasks being executed within a process of mutual adjustment, a management function becomes established which is responsible for coordination and control. A key challenge for management in commercial bureaucracies, therefore, is to nurture organizational commitment and, within the constraints of rules, procedures and specialized job roles, to encourage and sustain creativity (Guest, 1992). Without this there is unlikely to be constant innovation in the delivery of products and services to customers and other end-users. Herein lie the inherent contradictions of the commercial bureaucratic form of creative organization. It is the outcome of an attempt to apply the principles of administrative, retail and manufacturing organizations to those in which creativity is the core operational asset. It requires mechanisms to reconcile autonomy and indeterminacy with organizational control. One mechanism for obtaining the commitment of creative employees is to offer career paths within the context of relatively secure employment prospects. Formalized job descriptions organized within hierarchical reporting mechanisms offer, by definition, career routes. Employees are able to obtain promotion through 'exceptional' performance and, through this, their allegiance to their employing organizations will be reinforced. They will also perceive the employment relationship as long-term if their employing organizations offer careers with opportunities for personal progression. Accordingly, the employment contract will be regarded by both employer and employee as stretching beyond financial rewards to incorporate various psychological dimensions. These will include the opportunity to use the organization to express creativity. In other words, the commercial bureaucracy buys personal creativity and, in return for job security and promotion, it assumes that employees will put their psyche and their personal talents at the disposal of the organization for its general benefit. In this sense, there would appear to be a harmonious fit between the needs of employees and their employing organizations; the latter offer security and prospects in return for the acquisition of the former's intellectual capital.

However, there are usually countervailing tendencies. The tendency for commercial bureaucracies, through their dependence upon rules, procedures and task specialization, is to inhibit the realization of personal, intellectual capital. The psychological contract between employer and employee, instead of being based upon commitment, becomes defined in purely instrumental, pragmatic ways. Creative employees therefore conform to the requirements of management and, in this context, calculate how much creativity they need to expend to obtain the organizational rewards which are on offer. Since an employee's creative potential cannot be directly measured and since it can never objectively be determined whether a person's creative potential is being fully utilized, there is always scope for the creative employee to determine an appropriate level of intellectual or artistic output. Depending upon the extent to which they see themselves to be equitably rewarded, they are in a position to define the employment relationship. This can range from minimal and instrumental compliance to full psychological immersion in their job, involving full expenditure of their creative potential. Since the latter can never be measured, it is a source of indeterminacy and, hence, uncontrollable by management.

It is possible to identify three types of psychological contract: resentful compliance, instrumental compliance and internalized commitment. With resentful compliance, the employee's orientation will be 'grudging' and expedient. On the basis of his or her artistic and intellectual skills, the individual will work for a specific employer as a last resort strategy. For reasons which may be to do with age, geographical location or personal biography, the employee will define the psychological contract such that as little talent is expended as possible in exchange for what is perceived to be a minimum acceptable level of remuneration. Commercial bureaucracies are more likely to generate these attitudes among their creative employees. Their reliance upon formalized procedures and specification of work tasks is inclined to challenge the existence of work processes based on indeterminacy, autonomy and nonconformity. However, the numbers are likely to be small because such employees are unlikely to cope with this relationship for any significant period of time. Instead, they are likely to quit their jobs and to become freelance and self-employed providers of expert services. This allows them either to sell their skills to the highest bidder on a short-term, contractual basis or to trade in the market place by setting up their own independent business. Either option is relatively easy since virtually no capital assets are required for the purposes of trading. Earnings can be generated on the basis of technical, expert and intellectual skills in geographical contexts which, in the information age, may range from offering local to global services by marketing them through the internet and other channels of advanced technological communication.

Forms of commitment and compliance

As a result, employment relations in commercial bureaucracies are more likely to be characterized by instrumental compliance. There is less resentment and there are fewer attempts to expend the minimum amount of effort necessary, which as stated above is only likely to be a short-term, expedient employee strategy. Instead, creative employees will define the employment relationship in instrumental terms to the extent that they perceive their employing organization as a resource to be exploited for their personal goals. Because of the market reputation of their employer or as a consequence of the resources that it offers, they perceive opportunities for the pursuit of their occupational as distinct from their organizational careers. As the managing director of a large advertising company pointed out,

> People will stay in any place as long as they are getting out of that place what they want. Now, that's different things for different people. For creative people, if they can get very, very good work out and be well paid, they will stay. And most creative people would rather earn 50,000 a year for doing great work than 100,000 a year and be doing shit.

This touches upon an issue that confronts many organizations whose major assets are the scientific, expert, intellectual skills of their employees. What reward systems can they offer and how can they generate organizational commitment that will break down this essentially instrumental orientation? It is often the case that creative employees are highly committed to the task at hand because it allows them to develop their expertise further. But such commitment does not spill over to commitment to their employing organization. On the contrary, the instrumental compliance found among creative employees in commercial bureaucracies will be based upon three elements. First, personal reward systems and the extent to which these are equal to, or better than, those obtainable from other employers. Again the parameters of the relevant labour market will be highly variable and, depending upon employees' own personal circumstances, may range from a local geographical locality to a transatlantic or even global context. In the creative industries in Britain, it tends to be transatlantic in film, recorded music and television but more local in such areas as radio, the performing arts and publishing. But generally, in the entertainment industry, creative employees perceive themselves as operating within an English-speaking, global market and it is often personal circumstances that constrain their geographical mobility and, hence, job opportunities.

A second basis for an instrumental orientation, probably more salient than the first, is the extent to which the reputation of their employing organizations enhances their own professional status. Some organizations are perceived to be more prestigious than others. Some are seen as offering greater opportunities for developing personal creative skills, while others are regarded as having an international artistic profile, as being committed to higher standards of excellence, and so on. Such status hierarchies between organizations are, of course, a feature of the traditional professions such as medicine, the law, accountancy and academia. But it is equally the case in the creative industries. As stated earlier, an essential feature of creativity is its intangible indeterminate nature. How, then, can its quality be assessed? One criterion is evaluation by end-users and customers. In the case of the media, it is the various audiences who judge the quality of the products. But also, quality becomes equated with the provider of the services and hence a key method of differentiating between competing companies. In Britain the BBC, the ITV companies and BSkyB are perceived as offering different brands of programme although, in fact, many of them can be similar. Forms of output become associated with different types of company. This in turn spins off on to the reputation of the creative employees of each of these organizations. To work for the BBC is perceived to be more prestigious than to be employed by BSkyB. To be employed by the BBC bestows a measure of quality and expertise upon a creative employee's indeterminate creative skills that is not extended to those working for a satellite television company or Channel 5. This is analogous to working in the independent professions. To be trained at one of the London teaching hospitals, or with a City legal or accountancy practice, or to be an academic at Oxford or Cambridge bestows not only prestige but also competence upon those associated with these organizations. So, too, it is the case with creative corporations. To have obtained training or to be employed by one organization rather than another enhances an individual's occupational reputation, perceived intellectual capital and, therefore, a person's marketability.

If the reputation of employing organizations is an important factor in fostering an instrumental orientation among creative employees, a third factor is the resources which can be offered to them. Within increasingly international labour and product markets, those working in the creative industries are likely to shift between organizations according to the resources which can be offered to them for producing various cultural artefacts. It is not only the remuneration packages that enable companies to retain the services of television, record or film producers. It may be an important element but just as significant can be the resources which they are able to offer to allow them to produce quality and highly rated marketable products. Creative employees are thus able to enhance their personal reputations, both among their colleagues and their targeted audiences. A creative director in advertising observed that

> If you actually cut [the organization] down and box it off, in the way that many other industries, trades, whatever, are boxed off, I suspect you won't get the people, because the thing in order to work in advertising, with all its insecurities and other difficulties, is you need to be able to give people an extra edge ... I mean to be honest you're hoping for not so much a corporate, but I mean, a downright selfish attitude.

The resources of the organization therefore reinforce the marketability of a creative person's skills and, hence, the demand for their services. Being aware of this, companies will often offer contracts to lock in these skills if only for fixed periods of time. Even so, the outcome is likely to be reinforced instrumental compliance. This can become resentful if the contractual terms are later perceived to be inequitable. Witness the case of George Michael and Sony Records. This legal action – which was finally settled out of court – confirmed the essentially dysfunctional nature of resentful compliance among creative workers. George Michael refused to write and record new songs in accordance with his contract and there was very little that Sony could do. Instrumental compliance will be fraught with many tensions since both employer and employee will attempt to use each other for their own ends. This is less of a problem in manufacturing industry because employers, through the use of various management techniques and technology, have been able to remove the indeterminacy surrounding the execution of work tasks and hence, the control that employees can exercise over work processes. Where creativity is a core requirement, indeterminacy cannot be removed. The outcome is instrumental compliance with ongoing tensions surrounding employees' interpretations of their contracts, their remuneration packages and the availability of corporate resources for enhancing their personal reputations. The psychological contract between employees and their employers will be tenuous, with continuous negotiation over contracts, working conditions and the availability of resources. In other words, the creative employee's commitment to the organization will be low.

Cultural bureaucracy: internalized commitment

In commercial bureaucracies, these factors will undermine employees' internalized commitment to their organizations though not necessarily to the task in hand, their audiences, occupational reference groups or work colleagues. It is one of the great strengths of cultural bureaucracies that they are capable of cultivating employment relationships such that employees internalize not only the aims and objectives of the organization but also the means and 'ways of doing things' in order to achieve these objectives. This is often accomplished through extended periods of training, induction and mentoring and the offer of lifelong employment with steady career progression. The BBC, historically, was an organization of this kind. It was not only an employer but a 'club' to which selected recruits obtained membership and within which a particular set of attitudes and values prevailed. These emphasized the public service 'mission' of the BBC with its Reithian principles and provided a set of guidelines according to which tacit assumptions about quality programmes became established. As such, to be an employee of the BBC entailed a psychological commitment based upon the adherence to values that reflected those of the corporation. In short, to be committed it was necessary to fit in, to be a colleague who, through training, internalized the taken-for-granted value system. There was little need for control mechanisms of the kind often imposed within commercial bureaucracies because 'ways of doing things' were stipulated through custom and practice and internalized as part and parcel of the psychological contract.

Equally, internalized commitment is likely to be found in smaller and often recently founded creative companies. Employees in such firms are likely to have left larger companies – often because of their shift towards more formally bureaucratic procedures – in search of working environments more compatible with their understanding of creativity. By this they often mean employing organizations in which there is an absence of rules and regulations or a hierarchically structured management process. Work tasks are undertaken within a context of mutual adjustment, so that personal autonomy, indeterminacy and nonconformity are explicitly encouraged. In this sense, although the business may be a collection of individuals there is a shared commitment to a predominant set of values that dictates the specific cultural genre produced and what are regarded as acceptable procedures. Such shared commitment, which becomes psychologically internalized, is maintained by interpersonal collaboration on particular projects as well as through everyday working relations with the founder–owners or partners. Indeed, the employees of such companies are likely to have a stake in the ownership and to be closely involved with company strategy as well as with operational, task-orientated decision making. In a typical example from the music business, a finance director displays an attitude of commitment which is typical of functional as well as creative roles:

I have to work and bring my skills and my efforts in to something that I believe is worth supporting. I'm not saying that those [other] companies are not worth supporting. But, I actually believe that supporting the record company is worthwhile. For me personally, if I'm going to get up and work however many hours it is in a day, etc., I feel I want to do that for something that I believe is intrinsically worth supporting rather than some anonymous plc. I feel that working with everybody here is something that's worth spending hours, long hours during the day and on weekends, whatever, whatever the commitment takes. I think it is worth doing.

In 'alternative' media companies such as small independent record labels, underground magazines and book publishers, and radical film producers, internalized commitment is reinforced by employees' dedication to the statements and messages that their products attempt to sell. Indeed, it is this that constitutes the major reward for the intellectual effort expended. In response to a question about motivation, a publishing director states:

People work here because they want to. It's not the type of thing you work in because you want a job. You can work as much as you want to. I can think of a few people who haven't had a weekend at home in the past few months.

In these smaller creative organizations, whether or not they are committed to various alternative or radical goals, internalized commitment will be the predominant feature of the psychological contract because of the inability of such organizations to incorporate either resentful or instrumental compliance. Within the context of small-firm social relations, neither would be regarded as acceptable by fellow colleagues, founder owners or partners. If employees cease to be committed to the values and goals of their employing organization (and, hence, of their colleagues) they have little choice but to exit themselves. The result is that only employees who 'fit in' continue to be employed and, by assumption, employer–employee relations will be harmonious. If dissatisfaction is allowed to fester, this can affect the creative process and, hence, the performance of the small business.

If, then, small firms are characterized by internalized commitment, the psychological orientations of creative employees in larger commercial bureaucracies are typically those of either resentful or instrumental compliance. This is particularly the case in those commercial bureaucracies that have developed as a result of mergers and acquisitions within different sectors of the creative industries in the 1970s and 1980s. One result of this has been organizational restructuring. Commercial bureaucracies have been redesigned to foster a more congenial context for creative processes. The purpose has been to implement changes so that the psychological contract among creative employees shifts from compliance to internalized commitment. What exactly are these organizational remedies?

In essence, they involve measures to recreate entrepreneurial and small business cultures under the umbrellas of large corporations. The purpose is to reconstruct those features of small firms that are effective in nurturing creativity and high performance. Accordingly, new forms of commercial bureaucracy are emerging with organizational features different to those associated with traditional bureaucratic structures. Emphasis is placed upon breaking down the larger organization into a number of smaller autonomous operating units. Instead of creative employees reporting to departmental or line managers within hierarchical structures, they are given autonomy for strategic and operational decision making. Operational processes are devolved to project units, defined according to particular genres, products and market niches. Thus, large publishing companies will fragment their structures into various units for different genres of fiction and non-fiction books. Similarly, film companies will be structured according to different projects, while record companies will adopt labels that are targeted to different styles and markets for music.

The result is highly decentralized organizational structures operating units functioning as subsidiary companies, profit centres or as semi-autonomous project teams. In each case, the emphasis is to extend strategic and operational autonomy to those who are most capable of making decisions through their knowledge of products and markets. This encourages creative employees to utilize their intellectual capital to develop innovative cultural products in response to changing audience preferences. Within these smaller operational units, working relationships can be more personal and informal, based upon processes of mutual adjustment according to which the allocation of work tasks is undertaken between colleagues in self-managed teams. Collegiality makes it possible to avoid the formal roles and control relations characteristic of traditional commercial bureaucracies. If team leaders are respected because of their expert, intellectual and creative skills it is easier to share work responsibilities. In the absence of such expert legitimacy, the leadership role cannot be undertaken. The outcome is likely to be a deterioration in team dynamics, personal motivation and, therefore, of creative energy. Members of such operational units are likely to quit in such circumstances and to join competing organizations or set up as independent freelancers. If this occurs, it is likely to be by teams of colleagues rather than on an individual basis. This confirms the importance of mutual adjustment and the extent to which individuals are dependent upon each other for the exercise of their own creativity.

It would be a mistake to infer that such organizational forms are anarchic or unstructured. On the contrary, these operational units are tightly regulated in the sense that they stipulate quality standards and quantity of output. But this occurs without the exercise of traditional line management functions. How, exactly, does organizational control work in these devolved operating units? First, through time and financial budgets. Each autonomous unit is managed by setting the parameters within which, rather than the means by which, goals are achieved. The different operating units, through negotiation, are allocated financial budgets and given specified timescales within which projects are to be completed. Once these are agreed, each unit is given the autonomy to pursue its goals according to what it considers to be the most appropriate means for the task at hand. This is usually the outcome of discussion among colleagues about the most appropriate procedures. There will often be arguments and disagreements but consensus will normally prevail for fear that, otherwise, line management practices will be imposed.

The second control mechanism is through the measurement of outputs. While operational teams are given discretion as to how they produce, their outputs are precisely measured by corporate management. The overriding criteria will be such factors as sales volume, return on investment and market share. But equally, the reputation of the company will stipulate the required quality standards and the parameters governing the production of the particular genre. This leads to the third major control mechanism. With internalized commitment, as distinct from compliance defining the psychological contract, peer evaluation of the product – whether a television programme, a CD or a book – will be a key factor in stipulating the quality standards. This becomes internalized within the process of mutual adjustment and, hence, the day-to-day working relations between colleagues. Each has expectations of the other in terms of standards of performance, often expressed through concepts of 'professionalism' in the particular industry or sector. This constitutes a major source of informal control. Colleagues who are unable to achieve such standards will, through either explicit or implicit peer group pressures, exit from the group. If they choose not to do this voluntarily, their colleagues will freeze them out. This not only guarantees the maintenance of standards but also reinforces a process of self-governance whereby formally constituted, hierarchically imposed management processes are both inappropriate and redundant.

New forms of commercial bureaucracy, then, are emerging which attempt to overcome the motivational issues associated with more traditional bureaucratic forms. The aim of creating small, relatively autonomous operating units is to redefine the psychological contract so that internalized commitment prevails over instrumental compliance. In some senses, it is an attempt to re-empower creative employees – to extend their autonomy, nonconformity and indeterminacy – and to put them in control of operational work processes as in the case of cultural bureaucracies. 'New' forms of commercial bureaucracy impose greater psychological demands on their employees since they are expected to exercise creativity within a context of close interpersonal relations which dictate, through peer-driven pressures, their standards of performance. At the same time, they continue to be tightly managed, albeit indirectly, through the corporate measurement of their outcomes or outputs. Thus, tensions between corporate commercial goals and personal creative agendas persist, although in a different form. One solution for both corporations and creative employees is to transform this employment relationship into market-based relations – in other words, to reconstitute the creative work process according to market-based networks of purchasers and providers.

Network organizations

Network organizations are a growing feature of the creative industries. They can be either internal or external in how they operate. Internal networks are a feature of new commercial bureaucracies as discussed above. In these, senior management oversees a network of diverse subsidiary companies, profit centres and other devolved operating units. These, however, do not always function independently of each other. Often, there are internal markets with purchaser–provider relations between the different functions and resources that are needed to complete particular projects. The BBC has also moved in this direction in some spheres of its activities. According to this model, producers, for example, may choose technical facilities from competing operating units within the corporation. Equally, the services of technicians, creative experts and other specialists are purchased in-house. Through these means, an internal market is created with the organization functioning as a market place with tariffs and charges that regulate prices between in-house purchasers and providers. If particular services or resources are unavailable or the charges for them are too high, purchasers may then have the opportunity to acquire them from providers outside the organization in the external market.

The growth of this external market has provided the impetus for network organizations. Creative companies have not only decentralized and devolved their operating structures but have also externalized many of the functions that were previously undertaken in-house. Internal employment relations have been substituted by external market relations. In the initial stages this often occurs in relation to various support services such as cleaning, catering and maintenance tasks. But now, the shift has been to externalizing services and functions which, in the past, would have been considered to be at the core of a creative organization's strategic and operational activities. Many of them now depend upon networks of specialist providers for production activities ranging from sound engineering and post-production editing in television companies to many of the editorial tasks in book publishing. There is a long tradition of freelancing in the creative industries with performers, musicians and technical staff hired for the duration of particular projects, whether they be West End theatrical productions, films or series of concerts. But even so, there would be core staff employed on a relatively permanent basis. Today, many of these employees are out-sourced, with their skills purchased on a short-term contractual basis. Some ITV regional television companies provide clear examples of this trend. The outcome is organizations which may be described as flexible firms or, in the extreme cases, virtual organizations. They are slimmed down to a set of core tasks which are retained in-house with everything else subcontracted to external providers. There appear to be no guiding principles dictating this trend. It varies from company to company and according to criteria ranging from the personal philosophies of chief executives to cost considerations and the need to have (or not) exclusive access to particular creative talents and other expertise. Of course, the skills of network organization management are different from those required in the single bureaucratic type of organization. The management of external relations becomes as important as internal management.

A number of forces have encouraged network forms of organization in the creative industries. One factor has been the deregulation of labour markets in these industries. This has led to the ending of closed shops, the erosion of trade union influence and the dilution of employment legislation that, in the past, restricted labour mobility. Traditionally, trade unions enjoyed considerable bargaining power in the creative sector, even to the point of being able to hire and fire employees (as in national newspaper industry) as well as being able to negotiate job descriptions, working practices and reward systems. The negotiated outcomes were highly bureaucratized organizational structures in which there were often rigid job descriptions which restricted operational flexibility and internal (as well as external) labour mobility. The erosion of trade union power has enabled such traditional working practices to be abolished. At the same time, increasing competition in national, regional and global markets has forced companies to reduce their operating costs. They have been compelled to cut their overheads and to shift fixed to variable costs. The outsourcing of certain functions has been a major outcome because it is generally cheaper to buy in services and skills as they are required rather than to pay for them on a permanent basis, as with permanent employees. Equally, facilities or state-of-the-art equipment and technology can be more cheaply utilized by hiring from specialist providers than by having them permanently available for only intermittent use. Indeed, out-source providers can often develop higher levels of skills in their specialist areas than if these are undertaken within the context of larger companies. Smaller facilities management companies, in focusing upon particular kinds of technology provision, are probably more able to keep abreast of new technological developments than if they were located as a department within a larger organization. As the latter, they would have to bargain for their share of the organization's resources before they could use new technologies.

This leads to a further factor accounting for network organizations: developments in information technology. In the past, the growth of external networks was prevented by the need for those with creative skills to be instantly accessible. This could best be achieved by having them working within the same organization, as their activities could be coordinated and controlled through a work-based division of labour. With developments in information technology, it is possible to achieve a similar level of coordinated activity without the need for the physical proximity. The application of internet and intranet information systems enables tasks to be undertaken through a territorial rather than an organizational division of labour. This is particularly pronounced in the film, television and record industries where, increasingly, different parts of the production process are undertaken on a global basis. Within this territorial division of labour, work tasks can be executed in a more privatized, home-based manner, albeit within the context of virtual teams. In publishing and advertising it is becoming common for editors, copywriters and creative artists to work from home. Many of these will be corporate employees, but a significant proportion are independent freelancers who, with the use of PCs and ISDN communication links, are able to exploit their creative talents and input them into the relevant organizational processes, often more effectively than if they were working in the corporate environment. Indeed, the office or the workplace may cease to operate as the main locale for creative activity but, instead, become redefined as a place for meetings with clients and other project-based team colleagues. The execution of tasks through the utilization of personal talent is done elsewhere.

The limitations of information technology are less of a constraint on the further development of these networks than the attitudes of corporate managers and their fears of losing control over the means whereby tasks are executed. They are often reluctant to relinquish their management of day-to-day work processes. Generally, this is forced upon them by the need to cut overhead costs and salary bills and thereby they are compelled to outsource many core activities. The consequent emergence of the network organization constitutes a fundamental shift from the manufacture of creative products through employment relations to that of the market place. The management skills required, therefore, are those associated with these market relations – negotiating prices and agreeing contracts with various service providers. Such corporate managers, therefore, become responsible for managing external networks. The new commercial bureaucracy, then, is little more than a core of purchasers who negotiate contracts with a range of providers and are responsible for coordinating these services. Barnatt and Starkey (1994) have described developments in the television industry. Building upon the work of Miles and Snow (1986), they suggest that these external networks enable television companies to reduce their operating costs through pursuing four types of flexibility. These are numerical (staffing), functional, pay and technological. The outcome is a production core that coordinates four peripheral employment groups consisting of specialist freelancers, performing artists, contract service providers and facilities houses. Within the television industry, the processes of coordination often operate at the project level in the sense that productions consist of either one-off programmes or series. Thus, each project is, in itself, a self-contained work process, incorporating the coordinated activities of various freelancers over limited and temporary periods of time. These freelance experts are constantly grouping, disbanding and then regrouping, for the purposes of producing particular programmes. It is similarly the case in the performing arts, the theatre, film production and recorded music. What are the mechanisms determining this process of coordination?

Within a context of market relations and fixed-term contracts, the role of agents is pivotal. They fulfil key broker roles, bringing together purchasers and providers of different services. Agents are best known as representing authors and performing artists. But alongside these, the providers of specialist technical and creative services are continually having to market or promote themselves. This is done through nurturing personal contacts within industry-based networks. Hence, personal reputation is vital for obtaining work. But so too is the ability to work with others and to exercise personal creative skills in acceptable or compatible ways. As stated earlier, the work processes in creative industries are often based upon mutual adjustment. Therefore, personal compatibility is vital in a selection process that occurs among those offering their services as creative providers. It is this process which makes many sectors of the creative industries appear closed to outsiders, with recruitment based more upon 'who you know' than 'what you know'. Mutual adjustment requires both attributes and that is why networks in the creative industries are not based solely upon rational principles. Project leaders – whether they are in-house core purchasers or providers of services – will hire colleagues on the basis of personal qualities as well as experience, competence and cost criteria. This is recognition of how quality of output and cost-effectiveness is dependent upon the close collaboration of creative specialists involving processes of mutual adjustment.

It should not be assumed that networks consist solely of independent self-employed freelancers. The externalization of services has also led to the growth of small businesses. The creative industries are characterized by large numbers of small firms, often located in close geographical proximity to each other. How are these small businesses managed and are they faced with the same tensions in handling creative employees as their larger counterparts? As in large firms, creativity is the major asset. In order to avoid the perception of exploitation that creative employees often associate with large organizations, they are often offered a stake in the ownership of these businesses. Small firms in the creative industries are likely to be partnerships or firms of associates with all those who contribute to the performance of the business having a stake in the rewards. Such forms of business may represent support systems in which experience and skills are pooled. They are often established by disaffected creative employees who previously worked in commercial bureaucracies. As colleagues, they decide to quit their jobs and set up partnerships by pooling their financial resources and creative skills. Business partnerships also reduce the tendency towards organizational fragmentation. With stakes in the ownership of their business, employees are less likely to 'walk out of the door', creating vacancies within work processes which, because they are based upon close personal relations and mutual adjustment, are difficult to fill.

Network processes

What is distinctive about small firms in the creative industries is the attempt to avoid the organizational features characteristic of commercial bureaucracies. The emphasis is upon trust, informality, flexibility and cultures of participation in strategic and operational decision making. There is little in the way of a formalized management process. Controls are exercised through time and cost budgets within which projects have to be completed. Quality control and adherence to time schedules is often exercised through direct, face-to-face relations with clients and end users. Such controls are as tight as those in the new commercial bureaucracy although they are exercised through different mechanisms than those associated with traditional line management. Trust and internalized commitment are fundamental to these small businesses and they have no capacity to bear the costs associated with instrumental compliance and resentment. Relations among colleagues are necessarily cooperative and harmonious – despite day-to-day frictions and personal antagonisms emerging out of the need to accomplish complex, unpredictable tasks – since dissatisfied employees will quit.

A major challenge facing small creative firms is to manage business growth. How can these businesses be expanded without destroying their characteristics of mutual adjustment, high trust and informal working relations? How can tendencies towards bureaucratization be avoided? The answer offered by many proprietors is not to grow. Often this response is shaped by the personal experiences of working in commercial bureaucracies which led them to quit their jobs and to set up their own firms. In addition, they are often reluctant to expand because this would require them to devote a greater proportion of their time to administration and less to the exercise of their creative skills in relation to the production and delivery of cultural products and services. They are motivated by a desire to continue to exercise hands-on creativity and to keep their businesses small as a means for achieving this. Furthermore, as creative individuals, committed to the values of autonomy, indeterminacy and nonconformity, they often have little desire to manage other people.

Of course, some small firms in the creative industries do grow, eventually to become large corporations. The dynamics associated with this are complex. Suffice it to say that these are overwhelmingly the exception rather than the rule. The growth experienced by most small firms is likely to be extremely limited and often short-term. It is often a function of reaction to market demand rather than the outcome of an explicit strategy of growth. It might, for example, be the result of a client offering an additional, or exceptionally large, contract that then compels the business to take on additional creative staff.

In general, the situation of small firms in the creative industries is one of constant change. Employee turnover is high and they are very vulnerable to dissolution, acquisition and mergers. Freelancers will move between firms depending upon the availability of contracts and the financial rewards that are offered. Individuals may, within very short periods of time, shift from being employees in large commercial bureaucracies to becoming freelance, to setting up their own businesses, to dissolving these, to again becoming employees in large firms. These patterns of work are the outcome of the restructuring of the creative industries as market-based networks provide an alternative to in-house employment relations. Changes are not one-directional (Ursell, 1998). However, networks require individuals to develop portfolios of personal skills. Personal creativity and various expert and technical skills alone are insufficient. It is also necessary to be an effective negotiator to obtain good contracts with those who purchase services. Good interpersonal skills are also needed for cultivating and sustaining personal networks that are fundamental for ensuring that there are regular offers of work. The growth of network organizations has led to the development of attitudes among creative workers which emphasize market-driven self-reliance and independence – attitudes that are compatible with the indeterminacy, autonomy and nonconformity that are significant as features of creative work processes.

This chapter has described some of the directions of change that are occurring in the structuring of companies in the creative industries. It has focused upon the increasing role of commercial bureaucracies and network organizations and how shifts towards the former are also facilitating the growth of the latter. Furthermore, it has suggested that tensions within traditional commercial bureaucracies associated with tendencies towards hierarchical, line management practices have led to the emergence of new forms of commercial bureaucracy. In these, work process are organized around projects and employees are given operational autonomy within constraints imposed by time and cost budgets. As such, these organizations function as confederations of self-managing teams which are then assessed by corporate leaders according to various commercial criteria. Alongside this trend, and also driven by it, there is the growth of both internal and external networks such that traditional employment relationships are becoming supplemented by purchaser–provider market-based contracts. Such changes in organizational and working practices are, of course, occurring within a broader context of restructuring within the creative industries as these continue to become increasingly globalized in forms of ownership, patterns of management and, indeed, production practices. Such trends and how these are likely to affect future directions are the topic of the final chapter.

7

THE CREATIVE CHALLENGE

As post-industrial, information society develops, the creative industries are likely to assume even greater importance in the patterns of production, employment and consumption. Governments have begun to respond to this with policies designed to promote the sector (Smith, 1998) and international organizations have established similar initiatives (UNESCO, 1998). However, the creative industries will continue to change for a number of reasons. First, developments in information and communication technologies are likely to have a huge impact upon how cultural and media products will be manufactured, distributed and consumed. Convergence between different forms of information and communication technology will affect patterns of ownership, control and work organization as well as the market for the products of the different creative industries. Second, these industries are likely to become increasingly global, both in terms of their scale of operations and the markets for their products. Companies will be subject to greater competitive forces in the manufacture and sale of cultural genres, many of which will emerge and then evaporate as fashion and popular tastes in different countries change. Third, national and international regulatory frameworks will condition the future growth of the creative industries. But the existing frameworks will have to adapt to the opportunities and challenges generated by developments in information and communications technologies on a global scale.

The purpose of this chapter is to consider these issues. But before embarking upon this, it is useful to identify some of the *limits* to the organizational forms that exist within the different sectors of the creative industries. In their different manifestations, each variety of creative organization discussed – commercial bureaucratic, cultural bureaucratic, traditional/charismatic and network – is a response to, or even a reaction against, traditional forms of bureaucracy. It is this common feature that differentiates creative organizations from those that predominate in manufacturing, retailing and the service sectors. Since intellectual capital constitutes the core asset of creative businesses, processes of coordination and control are needed that avoid, mitigate or ameliorate the tensions associated with creative occupations. The four types of organizations reflect, and are a response to, these tensions. But all these forms have limits as modes of accommodation to the inherent problem of organizing creativity.

Some limits to different types of creative organization

In the 'new' forms of *commercial bureaucracy*, there is a limit to the extent to which activities can be outsourced and how far the remaining in-house functions can be organized on a highly fragmented, decentralized and devolved basis. There are problems of both internal and external coordination. In terms of outsourcing, there are a number of factors that need to be considered. If most expertise and creative talent is located 'outside' rather than 'inside' the organization, there is a risk that the organization will lose the opportunity to exploit innovative ventures and potentially profitable ideas. These can range from more fully utilizing developments in information technology to proposals for new business opportunities. When creative employees are working in-house, the organization has exclusive rights to their intellectual capital and property rights. When the creative process is executed through purchaser–provider relationships, the creative providers can sell their ideas, proposals and products in an open market. They can even be potential competitors should they decide to set up their own independent businesses for the purposes of exploiting innovative proposals. This is often what leads to the setting up of small independent television production companies, film facilities businesses and publishing houses.

At the same time, there are limits in the extent to which commercial businesses can rely entirely upon outsourcing and purchaser–provider relationships for the utilization of intellectual capital and creative labour. This strategy generates complex problems of coordination and quality control, as well as the problem of sustaining the commitment of creative providers to the values and ideals of the purchaser. Those who are selling their services independently on an open market will be constantly seeking new opportunities and their commitment to any commissioning organization will always be less than complete and, often, highly problematic. Different priorities in the scheduling of work, for example, can generate conflicts which purchasing organizations are unable to control. This will be the case particularly for those creative workers who are highly regarded in their relevant industry and who have well-established occupational reputations. Their position enables them to demand a high price for their services such that their charges or costs will be higher to any purchasing organization than if they were engaged in-house on a more permanent basis. This is why there are examples of companies, structured as 'new' commercial bureaucracies, which are bringing back in-house some of the activities they had earlier outsourced. In this way, they are able to regain control over work processes. For them, it is becoming apparent that mechanisms of coordination and control can be more effectively implemented through employment rather than market relations.

Cultural bureaucracies as organizational forms are also subject to growing constraints because of the increasing impact of a range of external forces. These are both politically and market driven. With the former, there are greater pressures for public accountability, with governments less likely to fund, for example, the performing arts without the commitment from publicly funded organizations that they can at least break even financially. Such pressure has ramifications for the internal structuring of the companies because tighter budgets constrain the resources available for artistic production. These, in turn, lead to restrictions in the autonomy of creative workers in terms of the parameters within which artistic creations are translated into performances, programmes and events for ticket-buying audiences. Some of the dilemmas of cultural bureaucracies are reflected in the changes that have been implemented in the BBC. The justification for the licence fee has to be in terms of the quality of the programmes that are broadcast as well as according to criteria of 'value for money'. Each of these is open to debate and each can be defined for decision-making or resource-allocation purposes in a variety of ways.

This is why commercial, market forces also pose a threat to cultural bureaucracies. If companies can produce television programmes, films and theatrical productions which are generally popular and therefore profitable, why should there be a need for state subsidy? Such questions compel all cultural bureaucracies to exercise tight controls over their costs because the profit-making sectors of the creative industries 'set the agenda' for the debate about appropriate levels of public funding. This is why, as discussed in earlier chapters, the pressure for cultural bureaucracies to take on the features of commercial bureaucracies have become virtually unavoidable in certain sectors such as television and radio broadcasting, film and the performing arts. This is a cause for much anxiety among creative employees and is widely interpreted by them as a threat to professional autonomy and 'artistic freedom' as well as to the national cultural heritage.

The limits to *traditional/charismatic* forms of organization are those associated with how far their culture, vision and mission can be sustained. These businesses are often established by relatively dominant personalities who have a clearly defined vision of how they wish to see their businesses grow. Small, family-owned publishing houses are perhaps the best examples. But this is also a continuing motive behind business start-up. For example, a recording studio may be set up to encourage the development of a specific genre of music, or a production company in the television industry may be designed to cater for a particular programme taste. On a larger scale, newspaper publishing has a long tradition of tycoons who have set up national and even global business empires to serve personal and political as well as strictly commercial ambitions. Their influence can extend across a broad spectrum of the creative industries.

But a key challenge facing such businesses is the extent to which the core values which sustain the culture and hence the motivation and enthusiasm of creative employees can be maintained in the face of three major challenges. The first of these is when the founder–owner(s) cease to be actively engaged in these businesses' day-by-day operations. They are often the personification or the representation of the organization's mission and values. The ultimate limitation on these businesses is the mortality of their founders. When they withdraw, there is often a succession crisis which the introduction of professional management has difficulty in solving. Express Newspapers, for example, never regained the vitality it enjoyed under the leadership of Lord Beaverbrook. Second, there are the problems of growth. As these companies expand, the need for operating procedures and reporting mechanisms – even if tempered by the need to accommodate the values and expectations of creative employees – is likely to dilute the original culture and mission. This is why many proprietors of such businesses choose *not* to grow, for fear that growth will destroy the business. The third challenge is that the *raison d'être* for the company's existence may cease to exist because of a change in the market place and the subsequent erosion of the niche which it served. Thirty years ago, feminist authors were unable to get their works published by the larger, established companies. Small feminist publishing houses were set up to meet the needs of these authors and their readers. Today, feminist literature has become incorporated within the lists of the major publishers, reducing the market opportunities for those small businesses earlier established. Of course, business opportunities are constantly generated so that traditional/charismatic forms of organization will continue to be a prominent feature of the creative industries. But they are highly vulnerable and, for the reasons stated above, likely to be targets for acquisition by larger commercial bureaucracies. In this way, the latter retain access to particular market niches, acquire product brands and intellectual property rights by purchasing such assets as back lists of books, and television or film archives.

Network organizations are subject to many similar limits. Often, they are based upon purchaser–provider relations that are regular and long established. Within these, business opportunities will emerge that will compel those who are self-employed to engage staff. As small businesses they can operate on the basis of mutual adjustment with each colleague having compatible technical, creative and personal skills. These businesses will be inclined to be self-sustaining so long as there is a regular and reasonably predictable flow of work. But should this increase, it may be necessary to develop a management process. This can lead to the removal of the founder–owner from the day-to-day execution of creative tasks and, as a consequence, changing the nature of interpersonal relations. Instead of the business operating on the basis of informal coordination, there can be a stronger tendency for the owners to exercise hierarchical and explicit control over the creative employees. This can lead to resentment and a decline in commitment towards the employing organization. In order to circumvent this risk, there is a tendency for those who have set up such independent businesses to trade as constellations of self-employed creative workers, the numbers of whom expand or contract according to the fluctuating demands for their services.

Each of the four types of organization, then, is characterized by distinctive limitations. Each possesses sources of tension and internal contradiction. Sometimes, such limits are overcome but more often they determine the parameters within which organizational strategies, company decision making and business development will operate. Each type of organization will be confronted with different problems as it competes in the rapidly changing markets that presently characterize all sectors of the creative industries. They do, however, share a common feature, in that each has to devise its own particular mechanisms for coping with the tensions associated with the management of creativity.

As stated earlier, for creativity to flourish such that organizations produce a constant stream of innovative products and services, it is almost a structural imperative to have work processes that allow autonomy, nonconformity and indeterminacy. Without these, those with intellectual capital will be reluctant to exploit their own personal creativity for the overall goals of their employing organizations. The fact that so many creative employees do frequently shift between employing organizations while others

155

set up their own businesses is testimony to the need for organizations to offer these capabilities. However, the inherent tendency for senior management to impose control relations of the sort associated with traditional bureaucracies inevitably leads to tensions which have to be accommodated through appropriate forms of organization design. If these are particularly acute within the creative industries, they are likely to become more pronounced across a wider spectrum of activities as economies take on features best described by the terms post-industrial and information society. These structural shifts are rendering obsolete many of the principles of hierarchical line management. A new and dominant paradigm of organization is likely to emerge as intellectual capital, comprised of those with various creative, expert and specialist skills, becomes the core asset of information-based businesses. Increasingly organizations will be compelled to find solutions and adopt cultures which accommodate autonomy, nonconformity and indeterminacy in the work process. A post-industrial management is likely to emerge to respond to these changing organizational features. But if such features become more apparent in most sectors of the information society, creative industries themselves will also change as a result of broader forces. These will be to do with technological changes, the continuing growth of global markets and the changing regulatory role of government.

Technological change

The creative industries have always been closely concerned with technology. While their output is expressed in terms of ideas, symbols, images and cultural forms, the means of production and conveying them to audiences have played a very important part in organizational structures and processes. The technologies of printing, telegraphy, sound recording, film and television broadcasting all supported new forms of organization, new genres of content and new audiences. It is to be expected that the creative industries today will be undergoing transformations linked with developments in technology. A number of important trends are in evidence.

As described in Chapter 2, the main sectors of the creative

industries have been differentiated historically by their core technologies, sources of finance and systems of regulation. The most significant current development in technology is the convergence between previously unrelated activities brought about by the application of information and communications technologies. These are the technologies associated with computing, telecommunications and broadcasting respectively – originally unconnected but now combined in increasingly close ways in the processes of production, control, transmission and reception of virtually all forms of media and organized creative output. The main engine for this process of convergence has been the microprocessor, the core technology of computing. Combined with transmission technologies such as fibre optics the traditional constraints on capacity and speed are removed. When all forms of information, whether numbers, text, sound or images, can be processed and transmitted in the same way, that is digitally, the traditional boundaries between forms no longer have fundamental significance. A television can become a computer terminal and vice versa, a compact disc can contain moving images as well as soundtracks, telecommunications links need not distinguish between voice, data or image signals. The convergence has been taking place at an accelerating rate since the early 1980s, when applications of new information and communications technologies began to spread wherever the gains in terms of speed and efficiency of processing were seen to have benefits. The internet is the most dramatic expression of the developments. In the creative industries, the advantages of the new technologies were perceived quickly. For example, in publishing and printing, electronic text processing and typesetting had replaced earlier generations of technology by the mid-1980s. The greater cost and complexity of image processing meant that developments in the audio-visual and broadcasting sectors were slower, but digital technologies are now widespread in the creation, manipulation, editing, and delivery of still and moving images to a wide range of audiences.

Arguably, creative workers have a particularly close relationship with the technologies they use; they are the necessary means of cultural production and they require high levels of knowledge, creative organization and skill. The creative industries are at the leading edge of new technology applications and the artistic

157

avant-garde often finds a creative stimulus in new technology. However, there are certain significant factors which inhibit convergence and restrict the development of new forms of creative organization. First, common technical standards and formats are needed in order for large-scale production and distribution to be possible, and for consumers to have products or services at appropriate cost. While digital technologies have clearly represented the way forward in all sectors, technical choices about systems, formats and modes of delivery have been more difficult to solve. The unsuccessful history of high-definition television (HDTV), notwithstanding substantial research and development, inter-industry cooperation and a sympathetic regulatory environment, as well as consumer interest, is a case in point. Between 1986 and 1992 the HDTV project was the leading research and development project within the framework of EUREKA, the EU research and development programme to promote new electronics industries. It was 'near-market' research designed to give European manufacturers an advantage in competition with Japan and the USA by establishing a new technical standard for television. It foundered on the clash between industrial and national interests as well as the rapid pace of technical innovation (Peterson and Sharp, 1998: 167–70). The music industry has been used to a succession of new sound recording technologies since the invention of the phonograph. It is now concerned not only with the traditional problem of applying a new digital technology of recording and playback to CD or DAT (digital audiotape) but also with music videos and delivery via the internet and home computers. Internet communications have so far resisted most attempts to bring them within the sphere of government regulation or commercial control. A full list of examples would show that the diffusion of new technologies throughout the creative industries has been uneven, lacking in coordination, and not always successful in its technical or commercial outcomes. Uncertainties surrounding the development of new technologies are, therefore, one of several important strategic questions which creative organizations face. A second factor which inhibits convergence is more directly linked with organizations as such. To the extent that they are bound up with prevailing technologies they are almost by definition ill-adapted to cope with innovations unless these are simply an extension to, or improvement on, what already exists. For example, to develop a line in educational multimedia products, a book publishing company would not only have to acquire relevant new technology but also new skill through retraining or recruitment as well as new styles of working and, possibly, management. In television, the spread of cable networks is led by organizations designed to create the infrastructure, market well-tried genres of programme, and attract and service subscribers. They are less well adapted to exploit the creative opportunities which the medium has opened up. Thus, there is a further strategic challenge to creative organizations to adopt the forms which are most appropriate to new technological circumstances. A third factor which inhibits the diffusion of new technologies, as well as convergence between them, is the nature and scale of the investment required. A generic technology such as digital processing is a simple enough concept which can be realized in a variety of settings as a solution to a specific technical problem. For it to become marketable as a mass consumer product or as a standard production technology, very substantial investments are required, usually involving cooperation between the largest firms. Only very few firms (for example, Microsoft in the design and supply of network access software) can seriously attempt to define the course of development on their own terms. It is more typical to find examples of collaboration between major players at the leading edge of technical innovation because the risks of investing ahead of the game are too high. Thus, for example, the BBC's strategy for entering the digital age in television has been to forge alliances with other interests. It also uses them to gain access to capital and commercial experience, while in return, other firms benefit from association with the leading television 'brand'. Smaller firms, unless they are deliberately seeking to profit from being the first among their competitors to exploit the advantages of new technology, are likely to delay investment until there is greater stability and predictability in the competitive environment. This is yet another kind of strategic decision which creative organizations – like most other commercial enterprises – routinely face. This is a suitable point at which to ask: how are the different types of creative organization likely to perceive and respond to these strategic questions associated with developments in new technology?

Among those organizations which are closest to the traditional/charismatic type, technology is unlikely to have a particularly prominent place in the vision of the founder or owner. They are creative organizations with a strong value orientation and a sense of cultural mission. Technology, which may be quite highly developed and up to date (for example, in an independent music company or publisher) is most likely to be seen as a means to an end, not an end in itself. The majority of such organizations are small- or medium-scale, so they do not include separate research and development activities. They will use technology which is standard in their sector of the industry, upgraded with some regularity and by incremental steps. Among the most traditional of these organizations, technology may be neglected at the expense of the original idea or value orientation, causing it to lose relative efficiency and thereby contributing to its commercial and cultural decline.

A cultural bureaucracy, typically a large-scale organization committed by law and convention to the goals of public service, including universal access and high technical standards, will have a different orientation towards technology. It is more than simply a means to an end, it is one expression of the core values of the organization. It occupies a permanent place in management strategies and there is a commitment to technical innovation through research and development. Thus, for example, the technical divisions of public broadcasting were responsible for a series of important technical innovations, such as 625 lines, colour, video, Electronic News Gathering (ENG), stereo and, most recently, digital television. Unlike some other large public insti-tutions, these cultural bureaucracies have systematically exploited new technologies as part of their wider cultural objectives. They are able to do this because there is a clear justification for the research and development activities from the framework of regulation and the system of funding. Any substantial weakening of the framework could, however, diminish the role of technology in the strategy of the organization.

A commercial bureaucracy in the creative sector will, by definition, have centralized mechanisms for strategic decision making. While technology certainly plays a part in strategic thinking, this dimension is expressed as part of the system of commercial priorities and competitive advantage, not as a value in itself. The problem which large creative organizations face, especially when they do not have their own in-house technical research and development operations, is the lack of expertise and technical foresight. For example, in publishing, music, commercial television and advertising, strategic decisions about technology are likely to be based on the advice of consultants, outsiders to the organization, who do not have close experience of its core creative processes. Of course, commercial bureaucracies have a tendency to use network organizations as a source for certain technical services which need not have a permanent place at the 'core', but this does not lead to a grasp of the 'big picture'. The growth of the new patterns of communication via the world wide web is a spectacular example of the importance of smaller organizations. Internet traffic generated by countless individuals and small businesses is driving the construction of the network, not the other way round. However, this is not to deny that some consolidation of businesses will occur as the web develops. At certain times companies have used strategies of vertical integration with equipment suppliers, production facilities or providers of value added services. It offers a solution to the problem of exploiting innovation but the 'solution' brings its own problems: the organization can become cumbersome and the technology or the facilities acquired may be a burdensome fixed investment.

Network organizations exist to provide specialized products or services within a cluster of similar organizations or in relation to larger, bureaucratic organizations. One of these specialisms may be in technologies for creative production. A network organization can develop a detailed knowledge of the technology, operational skills and familiarity with the needs of creative users without the 'distractions' of a complex structure. For example, the highly advanced technologies required for computer animation or computer-generated special effects are often found in small companies with the minimum of formal management structure. The combined business and creative strategy for such organizations is to exploit the advantages of being the most expert, most advanced and most original users of the latest generation of technology. While the objectives may be clear, it is a strategy with high risks. Advanced technology requires substantial investment, it can become quickly obsolete, it requires specialized expertise likely to be in short supply, and customers may be unaware of its potential. At the same time, network forms are too small to have control over the general trend of technology development. They must swim with the current and try to stay in the middle of the stream.

Strategies for maximizing creativity must therefore include technology, though there is no single 'best way' or formula to guarantee the outcome. Current trends in digital technology do, however, make it certain that the old boundaries between sectors of the media and creative industries will continue to be eroded, that opportunities for new formats, genres and audiences will stimulate the renewal of organizations, and that new organizations will enter the market. Of course, the rate of innovation and the scale of investment in new technology is closely connected with economic conditions on a wider scale. It is to these factors, especially the increasingly global nature of competition in the creative industries, that we now turn.

The globalization of competition

The enlargement of markets beyond national and even international boundaries has always been a feature of market capitalism. However, the trend towards 'globalization', as it is now popularly described, has accelerated during the late twentieth century and the processes include the creative industries to an increasing extent. Globalization is not a deliberate strategy, nor does it have inevitable consequences for organization. It encourages a perception of social relations and markets on a world scale but it does not automatically create a global culture (Robertson, 1992). For creative industries in particular there is a tension between the enlarged system of global social relations and the continuing need to articulate ideas, images and experiences to fragmented and complex audiences (Featherstone, 1995; Sreberny-Mohammadi *et al.*, 1997). Hence globalization is having a particularly important impact on those organizations – especially traditional firms and cultural bureaucracies – which have defined their creative objectives in terms of national culture, literary and linguistic tradition, or a national audience. Other types of organization such as cinema, recorded music, and advertising have operated in an international context since the origins of industrialized mass culture at the end of the nineteenth century. However, their operations have also become more globalized with the increasing scale and intensity of competition.

The BBC, the prime example of a cultural bureaucratic organization, has operated within a national context for most of its history, articulating national traditions, orchestrating public events, and providing the main platform for the mediation of politics and public debate. While it has an obligation to continue to meet these nationally defined objectives, it – like the publicly regulated commercial companies in ITV, Channel 4 and Channel 5 – is increasingly exposed to competition from commercial television providers whose strategies are international or global. They include satellite services that transcend national borders as well as multinational cable providers. These additional outlets represent a greater range and quantity of programme output, and therefore increased consumer choice. While the growth of new services has not diluted the audience for BBC programmes to the extent that some predicted, there has been steady erosion of its share. The need to protect the existing share of the audience and to compete for new audiences is one of the primary motives behind the move to a commercially orientated form of organization in the BBC. The strategy is not justified simply in terms of improving the competitiveness of national broadcasting in the name of greater accountability; it is a deliberate attempt to identify the organization as a global player (Birt, 1998). The BBC is a relatively large broadcasting organization by international standards, ranking eighth in the world by turnover among companies providing broadcasting services (OECD, 1999: 118). It has a very positive 'brand image' and archive assets and, rather like British Airways in the late 1990s, the Corporation is positioning itself for global competition to make best use of these assets. However, as a creative organization intimately connected with a particular language, history and culture, the BBC's response to international – essentially global American – competitive pressures will require new forms of organization which are likely to increase the inherent tension between commercial and cultural priorities.

Organizations of the commercial bureaucratic type are likely to have strategies for adapting to international competition. Many have an international, if not global, conglomerate structure designed to benefit from economies of scale in finance, production, coordination, distribution and marketing. All the world's largest media and entertainment groups compete aggressively through new technology, takeovers, low-cost manufacturing, standardized formats and strict financial control. In the popular media including films, television, video, recorded music and advertising, they are the dominant cultural intermediaries. However, there are some obstacles, even limits, to global organization of creative output. First, there are many examples of products, styles and formats which have 'failed' to communicate to international audiences. In advertising, for instance, where there is a very strong incentive to market mass products and services across the widest possible range of potential customers, the lack of a universal language, symbols or icons mean that local and national organizations retain an important place and may never be integrated with the global system. Second, there is the problem that, in many countries, the systems of commercial and cultural regulation which limit illegal copying or relaying of creative output in the developed western economies do not apply. To overcome the lack of regulation in some requires global cooperation between countries and industries. A third kind of limitation on global commercial bureaucracies is represented by the forms of regulation which states and international organizations can still apply. Examples include the attempts by the government in France to protect the national film industry against international, especially American, competition; the use of anti-trust legislation to oppose commercial monopolies in telecommunications and computer software; China's denial of permission to Rupert Murdoch to start satellite broadcasting in the People's Republic of China; and rules on cross-media ownership in the UK and many other countries. These systems of political, commercial and cultural regulation are themselves changing and they will be discussed in more detail below.

The consequences of globalization for other types of creative organization are more mixed. The traditional/charismatic firm, for example, may compete successfully on a local or a national scale, or in a single language area, by being responsive to traditions, styles, local movements and cultural trends which a global conglomerate would have no interest in unless they could be absorbed into a wider strategy. If a traditional firm does not have distinctive products or audiences of this type, and is selling to the same market as the large commercial bureaucracies, it will be vulnerable to takeover or closure. There are many examples of this in book publishing and advertising. The network organization has a different relationship to its commercial and cultural environment. It provides specialized products or services which depend heavily on personal contacts and complementary relationships within a cluster of organizations. There are likely to be benefits in geographical proximity – so, for example, the large majority of independent television companies are located in or near London – but there is no intrinsic reason why, with modern communications and new technology, some of these networks cannot be dispersed. Certain types of activity encourage clustering in those areas where there is a strong cultural dynamic at work related to the creative output: for example, fashion design houses in Milan, Paris and London (Bovone, 1994). Alternatively, there may be a local dynamic connected with specific linguistic and cultural minorities, such as the network of small television production companies supplying the Welsh fourth channel (S4C). The network organization competes with others in the same network, upon which it also depends, but has a subsidiary relationship to larger entities in the global system. They rarely compete in the same markets. However, there is a potential difficulty for network organizations which depend on the vitality of cultural minorities for their outlets. If cultural globalization continues to lead to the homogenization of popular cultural forms on a world scale through the spread of universal products, brands, formats and schedules, then network organizations may find their space for manoeuvre shrinking. On the other hand, there is good evidence to suggest that standardized, global output from multinationals co-exists with 'local' output (Scott, 1997). In this case, network organizations are unlikely to suffer serious decline, even in the context of global competition.

Regulating culture and creativity

During the 1980s and 1990s, Britain and most western European countries experienced a fundamental shift in political thinking about industry and the economy. As described in Chapter 1, this movement towards the 'liberalization' of finance, employment and markets had a profound effect on the creative industries as well as other sectors of the economy. At the same time as these developments on a national level, a process of institution building and reregulation has been occurring in the countries of the European Union and through international organizations such as the G8 countries, GATT and the OECD. They have significant implications for the structure and organization of the creative industries. It can be argued that there are two distinct processes at work. The first is the extension of markets, global logic and economic liberalism throughout the world, including countries of the former Soviet Union and its sphere of influence. This is reflected in the spread of capitalist forms of industry and organization but also in the structures of international cooperation and regulation which are designed to facilitate and encourage competition. Hitherto, the creative industries have been relatively neglected in these developments because of their small scale in relation to raw commodities and oil, steel and manufactured goods, and financial capital. In some contexts they have only recently been included in international discussions and agreements. However, the highly commercialized, global creative industries have become so important economically that they now have a natural place in these discussions. The main thrust is anti-protectionism, whether in traditional spheres or the creative industries, and the design of policies to encourage the opening up of new or existing markets. As far as the organizations described in this book are concerned, the main beneficiaries are the commercial bureaucracies which already compete openly in national and international markets. With the backing of international agreements and institutions they can operate with fewer restrictions even where, from a national cultural perspective, they are seen as an alien intrusion.

The second process affecting the creative industries in the UK is linked with developments in the European Union. In 1992, the competition policies of the EU led to the creation of the single

European market for goods and services. For the first time in the history of the EU, the creative industries were included in the sphere of economic regulation. This was consistent with the worldwide trend towards economic liberalization described above. However, in the case of the EU, policies on harmonization and the promotion of 'European culture' brought a new dimension to the structure of regulation. In the case of television – regarded as the most important cultural industry – the European regulations in the form of a directive, 'Television without frontiers' (European Community Directive, 1989), resemble national regulations but on a larger scale. The directive includes minimum quotas on home, that is EU, production; limitations on advertising; rules on content; and incentives for international cooperation within the EU. The effect of these and other regulations is to preserve a certain amount of space for the cultural bureaucracy within the wider context of international competition. Although the idea of European culture is implicit and undefined (Schlesinger, 1995) the premise of these regulations (as well as the national system of broadcasting regulation in the UK) is that the culture and creativity associated with the history and traditions of western Europe have value for the Union and require maintenance and a degree of protection.

The full organizational implications of the 'Europeanization' of the cultural industries are not entirely clear but a number of speculative points can be made. First, the pattern of growth of commercial bureaucracies shows that a number of large companies have expanded from an essentially national base through European mergers or takeovers to become European multinational conglomerates. Examples include Reed Elsevier (Anglo-Dutch) and Bertelsmann (German). They can combine strengths and compete globally from a European base. However, such organizations do not necessarily have immediate access to markets on a European scale because – from the cultural consumer perspective – those markets do not yet exist. The barriers of language, customs and culture have prevented television, publishing and advertising from extensive market consolidation. European co-productions in television have been few and often unsuccessful, and only a limited range of consumer advertising can be made for pan-European markets. There has been greater homogenization in products and formats which do not depend so heavily on national traditions and language – namely popular music radio recordings.

In the European context, where audio-visual media have had strong state support, national organizations are often among the largest operators in their national spheres. To the extent that they have moved in the direction of commercial bureaucracy as a result of reregulation and intensified competition, they are better equipped for survival in a more competitive environment, especially one which continues to be subject to a European framework of regulation. Thus, RAI in Italy, ARD in Germany, RTF 2 and 3 in France, all public broadcasters, have experienced loss of audience share similar to the BBC's and for similar reasons. They have all responded by adopting more commercial strategies. How far the process of commercialization will go is essentially a political question. Most states are not ready to leave the core creative industries – especially broadcasting, but also 'heritage', national theatre and opera – entirely to market forces. There are practical as well as aesthetic reasons for this. Governments depend for their support on news, information and opinion mediated by broadcasting. However, political authorities tend to seek the best of both worlds: control and accountability through the system of regulation, as well as commercial profitability. Organizations with some characteristics of the cultural bureaucratic type will therefore continue to play a leading part in the broadcasting sector under national and international regimes of regulation which will give them a measure of protection. But as organizations, they will be required to demonstrate their efficiency and accountability to the public by standard commercial criteria.

The framework of commercial regulation at the national and European level – through the Monopolies and Mergers Commission, cross-media ownership rules and European directives – is designed to promote orderly competition between firms and to prevent monopoly. This is usually seen as having particular importance in the information and creative spheres. As described earlier, the creative industries have, historically, displayed similar trends towards competition to those in other industries. Ownership, market share, and other measures of concentration show that a small proportion of firms account for a large majority of output and the logic of commercial bureaucracy is always to capture a larger part of the market through expansion, mergers and takeovers at the expense of competitors. Commercial regulation of creative companies does not as a rule directly address the cultural consequences of these moves – which may include reduced diversity of output, elimination of specific national or local forms – but only the economic questions such as access to the market, prices, or unfair practices. The cross-media ownership rules in the UK are designed to prevent overall control in closely related sectors. However, there is understandable concern among creative workers, the public and the regulators about the dangers of monopolistic control of information, ideas, forms of experience, as well as markets. From the perspective of the processes represented by the commercial bureaucratic type of organization, the threat of monopolistic competition is not simply one of standardization and the imposition of one type of product on a market, thereby eliminating choice. This is, of course, an important issue, as in the case of Microsoft computer software, or the political influence gained by Silvio Berlusconi through his Italian media companies, or simply the monopolies on advertising enjoyed by many local media. The broader question, which may also indicate a threat, is that these organizations explicitly prioritize commercial values and encapsulate creative processes in ways which lie well beyond the sphere of public regulation.

We began this book by remarking on the need for a more developed understanding of organizational dynamics in the creative industries and the post-bureaucratic era. We have offered an interpretation of the creative process in organizational settings and identified the organizational types and trends which appear to be most typical at the present time. It is a perspective which reflects the diversity of the world of work, organizations and management, as well as the variety of possible responses to the question of how creativity can be managed. The analysis has shown that new energies are released though a wide range of small organizations, through networks and through publicly subsidized activities. The public interest in capturing creativity for the maximum possible benefit to society and culture will be realized through a framework of regulation that continues to encourage these alternatives to commercial bureaucracy.

APPENDIX:
RESEARCH METHODS

This appendix provides a brief account of the research which is part of the background to this book. The present volume is designed to appeal to a wide audience and is not a detailed report of the research as such. Empirically based studies of occupations and organizations in the creative sector have been relatively rare, so it may be of interest to some readers to have details of the aims and methodology of the project. The overall objectives of the research, which was funded by the Economic and Social Research Council (R-000-23-2352) and entitled 'Organizational Design and the Management of Creative Employees', were to identify and examine the most significant varieties of managerial strategy, organizational process and employee dynamics within a range of media and creative industries. All these industries have been experiencing changes consequent upon the development of new production technologies, mergers and takeovers, the emergence of new single- or multimedia markets, or the scaling down of public subsidies, and the last two decades have seen particularly rapid change and restructuring. From the perspective of social theories of the 'information society', as well as theories of management and organizational behaviour, these changes presented a challenge: would the evidence and observation of organizational practices confirm their often sweeping generalizations?

Appendix: research methods

The research design was a compromise between a large-scale survey of the entire range of creative organizations on the one hand, and selected case studies on the other. The data from the investigation was intended to be broadly representative of the range and variety of activities in the UK rather than an exhaustive description. In fact, the boundaries of the 'creative' industries are difficult to define, since organizational creativity is present to some degree in many other sectors, including public relations, retailing, education, tourism and even manufacturing. The research therefore concentrated on a number of 'core' creative areas, namely broadcasting, publishing, the recorded music industry, advertising, and the performing arts. The broadcast media – television and radio – were included because of their centrality to national culture and also because they embody the processes of transformation of the 'public service' media. In the BBC and the ITV companies, the data collection focused on the production of drama series and serials in order to highlight the processes of artistic and cultural creativity in their organizational context. The film industry was not examined separately but the research included independent television and film production companies whose activities illustrate the current convergence between the two sectors. The research in radio likewise included both BBC and ILR personnel working in the regions as well as London. The selection of book publishers was designed to bring out contrasts between large, multinational corporations and smaller publishing houses, mostly in the field of fiction publishing. The interviews in the recorded music industry and in advertising agencies reflected a similar contrast between the dynamics of large and small firms. The performing arts, both 'commercial' and publicly subsidized, were included because the production of live performances involves particular problems of creative organization. While the research does not claim to be based on a representative sample of employees in the creative industries, the data can be said to relate to the most significant problems of creative organizations in these industries, whether in public or private corporations, large- or small-scale organizations, or in different types of media.

Three types of data were collected. The first was documentary data, published and unpublished, including company reports, business news coverage, organization charts, job descriptions, employment data, and in-house communications. Second, semi-structured interviews were conducted with managers and creative staff. There were few problems of access or confidentiality, although this proved to be slightly more difficult in the music industry than elsewhere – possibly because of the adverse attention it sometimes receives from the popular music press. A third source of data was detailed observation of two BBC television drama productions in the making. In each case, a researcher spent one week on site with the production team, observing and conducting informal interviews, collecting evidence for two case studies, one in a studio context, the other involving location filming.

In total, 114 interviews were conducted, each lasting typically one hour or more. These were tape recorded, transcribed and formatted for qualitative data analysis. The approach was semi-structured, using common headings and themes, while allowing for more detailed elaboration according to the specific context of the organization or the role of the interviewee. When interviewees are quoted, they are identified by their organization and function, rather than in person. The anonymity is designed to focus attention away from personalities and on the organizational issues and is not necessarily used because the interviewees wished to keep their remarks confidential. For the analysis of this data, the computer software package QSR NUD*IST (Non-Numerical Unstructured Data Indexing, Searching and Theory-building) was used to explore themes such as 'bureaucracy', 'autonomy', 'control' and, of course, 'creativity'. This was particularly helpful for discovering connections and making comparisons between the different creative sectors.

In several of the above chapters, data from the study have been used to illustrate the general argument. Any particular item of data is, of course, open to more than one interpretation, especially when the context is not fully visible. And many generalizations are not fully backed by evidence in the text, for reasons of length. However, the evidence which is offered here, as well as being part of a more detailed empirical study, gains strength from the fact that, almost without exception, the respondents recognized the pertinence of the research questions to their work and managerial responsibilities.

REFERENCES

Adorno, T.W. (1991) *The Culture Industry: Selected Essays on Mass Culture*, edited by J-M. Bernstein. London: Routledge.

Advertising Association (1998) *Advertising Statistics Yearbook*. Henley on Thames: NTC Publications.

Alvesson, M. (1993) *Cultural Perspectives on Organizations*. Cambridge: Cambridge University Press.

Baines, S. (1999) Servicing the media: Freelancing, teleworking and 'enterprising' careers. *New Technology, Work and Employment*, 14(1), 18–31.

Barnatt, C. and Starkey, K. (1994) The emergence of flexible networks in the UK television industry. *British Journal of Management*, 5, 251–60.

Birt, J. (1998) 75 Years of the BBC. Lecture to mark the 75th anniversary of the BBC, Institution of Electrical Engineers, London, 21 January.

Blumler, J.G. and Spicer, C.M. (1990) Prospects for creativity in the new television marketplace: Evidence from program-makers. *Journal of Communication*, 40(4), 78–101.

Boden, M.A. (1990) *The Creative Mind: Myths and Mechanisms*. London: Weidenfeld and Nicolson.

Bourdieu, P. (1993) *The Field of Cultural Production: Essays on Art and Literature*. Cambridge: Polity.

Bovone, L. (ed.) (1994) *Creare communicazione. I nuovi intermediari di cultura a Milano*. Milan: Franco Angeli.

BPI Ltd (1995) *Statistical Handbook 1995*. London: British Phonographic Institute.

Managing creativity

Braverman, H. (1974) *Labor and Monopoly Capital: The Degradation of Work in the Twentieth Century*. New York, NY: Monthly Review Press.

Brown, P. and Scase, R. (1994) *Higher Education and Corporate Realities*. London: UCL Press.

Burns, T. (1977) *The BBC: Public Institution and Private World*. London: Macmillan.

Burns, T. and Stalker, G.M. (1994) *The Management of Innovation*, Revised edition. Oxford: Oxford University Press.

Burrage, M. and Torstendahl, R. (eds) (1990) *Professions in Theory and History: Rethinking the Study of Professions*. London: Sage.

Burrell, G. and Morgan, G. (1979) *Sociological Paradigms and Organizational Analysis: Elements of the Sociology of Corporate Life*. London: Heinemann.

Castells, M. (1996) *The Rise of the Network Society*. Oxford: Blackwell.

Central Statistical Office (1995) *Social Trends*, 25th edition. London: HMSO.

Chattell, A. (1998) *Creating Value in the Digital Era*. London: Macmillan.

Clark, G. (1988) *Inside Book Publishing*. London: Blueprint.

Clegg, S.R. (1990) *Modern Organizations: Organization Studies in the Postmodern World*. London: Sage.

Coser, L., Kadushin, C. and Powell, W. (1981) *Books: The Culture and Commerce of Publishing*. New York, NY: Basic Books.

Crozier, M. (1964) *The Bureaucratic Phenomenon*. London: Tavistock.

Daymon, C. (1997) Making sense of Meridian: A cultural analysis of organisational life in a new television station. Unpublished PhD thesis, University of Kent at Canterbury.

Dominick, J.R. and Pierce, M.C. (1976) Trends in network prime time programming 1953–74. *Journal of Communications*, 261, 70–80.

Du Gay, P. (1996) Making up managers: Enterprise and the ethos of bureaucracy, in S.R. Clegg and G. Palmer (eds) *The Politics of Management Knowledge*. London: Sage.

Elliott, P. (1972) *The Making of a Television Series: A Case Study in the Sociology of Culture*. London: Constable.

Elliott, P. (1977) Media organizations and occupations: An overview, in J. Curran, M. Gurevitch and J. Woollacott (eds) *Mass Communication and Society*. London: Edward Arnold.

Ettema, J.S. and Whitney, D.C. (eds) (1982) *Individuals in Mass Media Organisations*. London: Sage.

European Community Directive (1989) Television without frontiers. *Official Journal of the European Communities*, No. L298/23, October 17.

Feather, J. (1993) Book publishing in Britain: An overview. *Media, Culture and Society*, 15(2), 167–81.

Featherstone, M. (1995) *Undoing Culture: Globalization, Postmodernism and Identity*. London: Sage.

References

Fletcher, W. (1990) *Creative People: How to Manage Them and Maximize Their Creativity*. London: Century Hutchinson.

Francis, A. (1986) *New Technology at Work*. Oxford: Clarendon Press.

Frost, P., Moore, L., Louis, M., Lundberg, C. and Martin, J. (eds) (1991) *Reframing Organisational Culture*. Newbury Park, CA: Sage.

Garnham, N. (1990) *Capitalism and Communication: Global Culture and the Economics of Information*. London: Sage.

Goffee, R. and Scase, R. (1995) *Corporate Realities: The Dynamics of Large and Small Organizations*. London: Routledge.

Goss, D. (1991) *Small Business and Society*. London: Routledge.

Granger, B., Stanworth, J. and Stanworth C. (1995) Self-employment career dynamics: The case of 'unemployment push' in UK book publishing. *Work, Employment and Society*, 9(3), 499–516.

Guest, D. (1992) Employee commitment and control, in J.F. Hartley and G.M. Stephenson (eds) *The Employment Relation: The Psychology of Influences and Control at Work*, pp. 111–36. Oxford: Blackwell.

Hassard, J. and Parker, M. (eds) (1993) *Postmodernism and Organizations*. London: Sage.

Hennion, A. (1983) Music industries and creativity, in Council of Europe. *The Place of Small Firms in the Record Industry and their Role in Musical Creativity*. Strasbourg: Council of Europe.

Henry, J. and Walker, D. (eds) (1991) *Managing Innovation*. London: Sage.

Hesmondhalgh, D. (1996) Flexibility, post-Fordism and the music industries. *Media, Culture and Society*, 18(3), 469–88.

Hirsch, P.M. (1972) Processing fads and fashions: an organisation-set analysis of cultural industry systems. *American Journal of Sociology*, 77(4), 639–59.

Hirsch, P.M. (1978) Production and distribution roles among cultural organizations: On the division of labor across intellectual disciplines. *Social Research*, 45(2), 315–30.

Hirsch, P.M. (1985) U.S. cultural productions: The impact of ownership. *Journal of Communication*, 35(3), 110–21.

Institute for Employment Research (1998) *Review of the Economy and Employment 1997/98*. University of Warwick.

Joas, H. (1996) *The Creativity of Action*. Cambridge: Polity.

Johnson, T.J. (1972) *Professions and Power*. London: Macmillan.

Kanter, R.M. (1983) *The Change Masters*. London: George Allen and Unwin.

Koestler, A. (1964) *The Act of Creation*. London: Hutchinson.

Kumar, K. (1975) Holding the middle ground: The BBC, the public and the professional. *Sociology*, 9(1), 67–88.

Lash, S. and Urry, J. (1994) *Economies of Signs and Space*. London: Sage.

Legge, K., Clegg, C.W. and Kemp, N.J. (eds) (1991) *Case Studies in*

Information Technology: People and Organizations. Oxford: NCC Blackwell.

Leiss, W., Kline, S. and Jhally, S. (1986) *Social Communication in Advertising*. London: Methuen.

LeMahieu, D.L. (1988) *A Culture for Democracy: Mass Communication and the Cultivated Mind in Britain between the Wars*. Oxford: Clarendon.

Lockwood, D. (1964) Social Integration and System Integration, in G.K. Zollschan and W. Hirsch (eds) *Explorations in Social Change*. London: Routledge.

Lopes, P.D. (1992) Innovation and diversity in the popular music industry, 1969–1990. *American Sociological Review*, 57(1), 56–71.

Lyon, D. (1986) From 'post-industrialism' to 'information society': A new social transformation? *Sociology*, 20, 577–88.

McCourt, T. and Rothenbuhler, E. (1997) SoundScan and the consolidation of control in the popular music industry. *Media, Culture and Society*, 19(2), 201–18.

McKinlay, A. and Quinn, B. (1999) Management, technology and work in commercial broadcasting, c. 1979–98. *New Technology, Work and Employment*, 14(1), 2–17.

Maslow, A. (1962) *Towards a Psychology of Being*. Princeton, NJ: D. Van Nostrand Co. Inc.

Mattelart, A. (1991) *Advertising International: The Privatisation of Public Space*. London: Comedia/Routledge.

Mayo, E. (1975) *The Social Problems of an Industrial Civilization*. London: Routledge and Kegan Paul.

Miège, B. (1987) The logics at work in the new cultural industries. *Media, Culture and Society*, 9(3), 273–89.

Miège, B. (1989) *The Capitalization of Cultural Production*. International General.

Miège, B., Panjon, P. and Salaun, J-M. (1986) *L'industrialisation de l'audio-visuelle: des programmes pour les nouveaux médias*. Paris: Aubier.

Miles, R.E. and Snow, C.C. (1986) Organizations. New concepts for new forms. *California Management Review*, XXVII, 62–73.

Mintzberg, H. (1983) *Structures in Five: Designing Effective Organisations*. Englewood Cliffs, NJ: Prentice Hall.

Morgan, G. (1986) *Images of Organisation*. London: Sage.

Morgan, G. (1989) *Creative Organization Theory: A Resourcebook*. London: Sage.

Murdock, G. (1990) Redrawing the map of the communications industries: Concentration and ownership in the era of privatization, in M. Ferguson (ed.) *Public Communication – The New Imperatives: Future Directions for Media Research*. London: Sage.

References

Murdock, G. and Golding, P. (1977) Capitalism, communication and class relations, in J. Curran, M. Gurevitch and J. Wollacott (eds) *Mass Communications and Society*, pp. 12–43. London: Edward Arnold.

Myerscough, J. *et al.* (1988) *The Economic Importance of the Arts*. London: Policy Studies Institute.

Negus, K. (1992) *Producing Pop: Culture and Conflict in the Popular Music Industry*. London: Edward Arnold.

Negus, K. (1995) Where the mystical meets the market: commerce and creativity in the production of popular music. *Sociological Review*, 43(2), 316–41.

Negus, K. (1996) *Popular Music in Theory: An Introduction*. Cambridge: Polity.

Negus, K. (1998) Cultural production and the corporation: Musical genres and the strategic management of creativity in the US recording industry. *Media, Culture and Society*, 20(3), 359–79.

Neumann, W.R. (1991) *The Future of the Mass Audience*. Cambridge: Cambridge University Press.

OECD (1999) *Communications Outlook 1999*. Paris: OECD.

Office for National Statistics (1998) *Britain 1999: The Official Yearbook of the United Kingdom*. London: The Stationery Office.

Peters, T. (1987) *Thriving on Chaos: A Handbook for a Management Revolution*. London: Macmillan Alfred A. Knopf.

Peterson, R. and Berger, D. (1975) Cycles in symbol production: The case of popular music. *American Sociological Review*, 40, 158–73.

Peterson, J. and Sharp, M. (1998) *Technology Policy in the European Union*. Basingstoke: Macmillan.

Pilati, A. (ed.) (1993) *Mind: Media Industry in Europe*. Milan: MIND Institute of Media Economics/London: John Libbey.

Policy Studies Institute (1986–98) *Cultural Trends* (Annual). London: PSI.

Ray, L. and Reed, M. (eds) (1994) *Organizing Modernity: New Weberian Perspectives on Work, Organization and Society*. London: Routledge.

Reich, R. (1992) *The Work of Nations*. New York, NY: Vintage Books.

Ritzer, G. (1993) *The McDonaldization of Society: An Investigation into the Changing Character of Contemporary Social Life*. Newbury Park, CA: Pine Forge Press.

Robertson, R. (1992) *Globalization: Social Theory and Global Culture*. London: Sage.

Robinson, S.L., Kraatz, M.S. and Rousseau, D.M. (1994) Changing obligations and the psychological contract: A longitudinal study. *Academy of Management Journal*, February, 137–52.

Rogers, C.R. (1961) *On Becoming a Person*. London: Constable.

177

Rothenbuhler, E.W. and Dimmick, J.W. (1982) Popular music: Concentration and diversity in the industry 1974–1980. *Journal of Communication*, 32, 143–7.

Saundry, R. (1998) The limits of flexibility: The case of UK television. *British Journal of Management*, 9, 151–62.

Saundry, R. and Nolan, P. (1998) Regulatory change and performance in TV production. *Media, Culture and Society*, 20(3), 409–26.

Scannell, P. (1991) *A Social History of Broadcasting: Volume One 1922–1939. Serving the Nation*. Oxford: Blackwell.

Schlesinger, P. (1995) *Europeanisation and the Media: National Identity and the Public Sphere*. Working paper no. 7/95. Oslo: ARENA.

Scott, A. (ed.) (1997) *The Limits of Globalization: Cases and Arguments*. London: Routledge.

Sierz, A. (1997) British theatre in the 1990s: A brief political economy. *Media, Culture and Society*, 19(3), 461–9.

Smith, C. (1998) *Creative Britain*. London: Faber and Faber.

Sreberny-Mohammadi, A., Winseck, D., McKenna, J. and Boyd-Barrett, O. (eds) (1977) *Media in Global Context: A Reader*. London: Edward Arnold.

Straw, W. (1993) Characterising rock music culture: The case of heavy metal, in S. During (ed.) *The Cultural Studies Reader* pp. 368. London: Routledge.

Taylor, F.W. (1972) *Scientific Management*. Westport, CT: Greenwood.

Thompson, J.B. (1995) *The Media and Modernity: A Social Theory of the Media*. Cambridge: Polity Press.

Tracey, M. (1998) *The Decline and Fall of Public Service Broadcasting*. Oxford: Oxford University Press.

Tunstall, J. (1993) *Television Producers*. London: Routledge.

Tunstall, J. and Palmer, M. (1991) *Media Moguls*. London: Routledge.

Twiss, B. (1986) *Managing Technological Innovation*. Harlow: Longman.

UNESCO (1998) *World Culture Report: Culture, Creativity and Markets*. Paris: UNESCO.

Ursell, G. (1998) Labour flexibility in the UK commercial television sector. *Media, Culture and Society*, 20(1), 129–53.

Varlaam, C., Leighton, P., Pearson, R. and Blum, S. (1990) *Skill Search: Television, Film and Video Industry Employment Patterns and Training Needs*. Brighton: Institute of Manpower Studies.

Weber, M. (1978) *Economy and Society*, Vols 1 and 2, edited by G. Roth and C. Wittich. Los Angeles, CA: University of California Press.

Webster, F. (1995) *Theories of the Information Society*. London: Routledge.

INDEX

Adorno, T., 26, 34
advertising
    industry trends, 45–7
    managerial control, 91–4
    output, 33
    see also division of labour
agents, 146
Arts Council, 30, 47, 50n
authenticity, 3
autonomy, viii, 19–21, 56, 71–2, 80

Baines, S., 53
bargaining, 17, 143
    see also trade unions
Barnatt, C., 145
BBC, 25, 28, 32, 38, 55–9, 72–3,
        100–1, 136–7, 159, 163
    see also Producer Choice
Birt, J., 163
Boden, D., 18
Bourdieu, P., 54
Bovone, L., 54, 165
Braverman, H., 12, 16
broadcasting
    independent production, 39, 75,
        101, 114

public service, 28, 38, 40, 50n
technology, 158–60
see also BBC; radio; television
Broadcasting Act, 1990, 38, 40,
        50n, 114
Brown, P., 4
bureaucracy
    characteristics of, 4–6
    costs of, 8
    culture of, 7, 74, 130
    debureaucratization., 10
    limits of, 15, 74, 79–83, 151
    see also commercial bureaucracy;
        cultural bureaucracy
bureaucratic personality, 6
Burns, T., 18, 29, 38, 56, 72
Burrage, M., 72
Burrell, G., 12

careers, 43, 131
Castells, M., 9
charisma, 100, 112, 123
charismatic organization, *see*
        traditional organization
Chattell, A., 10
Clark, G., 42

179

Clegg, S., 5
commercial bureaucracy, 98–9, 129–36, 151–2
commercial model, 25, 27–8
commitment, 8, 97, 106, 119–20, 132, 137–9
    see also psychological contract
compliance
    instrumental, 133–6
    resentful, 132–3
    see also commitment
concentration
    format, 34–5
    ownership, 34–5, 41–4, 46–7, 168–9
    product, 34
    see also conglomerates
conglomerates, 36, 44–5, 64, 164, 167
control, 54–5, 83, 94, 96–102
coordination, 52, 54–5, 94–6
Coser, L., 85
creative industries
    characteristics of, vii–ix, 23
    diversity of, 26
    emergence of, 25, 28
    employment, 31–2, 44–5
    export value of, 24
    management within, 13, 71–6
    regulation of, 165–9
    studies of, 12–13, 50n
    see also commercial model; skills; subsidy
Creative Industries Taskforce, 24, 45
creativity
    concepts of, 3, 18
    contra-positioning with management, 2–3, 7
    definition of organizational creativity, 19–20, 94
    and freedom, 3
    in manufacturing organizations, viii–ix, 4, 18, 37
    personal creativity, 16, 18–19
Crozier, M., 17

cultural bureaucracy, 29, 38, 56–8, 72, 80, 100–1, 116, 119, 152–3
cultural intermediaries, 54, 63
culture
    corporate culture, 8
    European, 167
    mediazation of, 24
    of organizations, 19, 78–9, 102n, 111, 139
culture industry, 26, 34

DAT (digital audio tape), 158
Daymon, C., 50n, 59
deskilling, 16–17, 59–60
division of labour
    in advertising, 67–9
    in book publishing, 62–5
    in creative industries 16–17, 19
    in music, 65–7
    in performing arts, 69–71
    in radio, 60–2
    in television, 38, 55–60
Du Gay, P., 18

editor, 62–5, 110
enterprise webs, 9
Ettema, J., 12
European Directive, 38, 167

Feather, J., 42
Featherstone, M., 162
film
    audiences, 33
    industry structure, 31
Fletcher, W., 19
flexible firm, 143, 145
    see also outsourcing
Fordism, 5, 12
Francis, A., 17
freelance, 2–3, 32, 37, 43, 59, 63, 76, 122, 145–6

Garnham, N., 13
globalization, 162–5

Index

Goffee, R., 12
Goss, D., 8
Granger, B., 43
Guest, D., 131

Hassard, J., 5
HDTV (high-definition television),
    158
Hennion, A., 44
Henry, J., 18
Hesmondhalgh, D., 44
Hirsch, P., 26, 43

IBA, 38, 50n
independence, see autonomy
indeterminacy, viii, 13, 16, 20–1, 54,
    72, 80, 132
information society
    characteristics of, vii–viii, 4
    concept of, 21n
    see also occupations
information technology, 9, 17, 37,
    144–5, 156–62
ITV, 38–9, 114, 130, 143, 163

Japanese management, 3
Joas, H., 18
Johnson, T., 72

Kanter, R., 5
Koestler, A., 18
Kumar, K., 100

Lash, S., 9
LeMahieu, D., 29
Legge, K., 17
Leiss, W., 46
licence fee, 25, 28–9
Lockwood, D., 103n
Lopes, P., 35

management theory, 3, 12
managerialism, 7, 65, 120
McDonaldization, 6

McKinlay, A., 38
Maslow, A., 18
Mattelart, A., 46
Mayo, E., 3
Miège, B., 50n
Miles, R., 145
Mintzberg, H., 14
Morgan, G., 3, 8, 12, 18
motivation, see commitment
Murdock, G., 13, 34
music industry, 35–6, 44–5, 65–7
    see also division of labour
mutual adjustment, 14–16, 124,
    137, 140, 146
Myerscough, J., 47

National Lottery, 30
Negus, K., 44, 67
network organization, 10, 46, 59,
    67, 101–2, 102n, 121–4, 142–7,
    154–5, 165
Neumann, W., 34
nonconformity, viii, 20–1, 72

occupations
    decline in manufacturing, 10–11
    growth in services, 1–2, 10–11
organizational culture, see culture
outsourcing, 10, 145, 151–2
ownership
    moguls, 27–8, 36
    publishing 27
    radio, 40
    small businesses, 146–7
    see also concentration

performing arts
    industry trends, 47–8, 168
    managerial control, 88–91
    see also subsidy; division of labour
Peters, T., 5
Peterson, J., 158
Peterson, R., 35
Pilati, A., 47

post-industrial society
  characteristics of, 1–2, 21–2
  concept of, 21n
  occupations, 1–2, 4
  see also information society;
    occupations
producer, 57–8, 72, 116
Producer Choice, 39, 114, 122,
  128n, 142
Producers' Guidelines, 81
professions, 103n, 134–5
professionalism, 72, 141
project organization, 15–16, 46
proprietors, *see* ownership
psychological contract, 97, 129–33
publishing
  feminist, 154
  industry trends, 41–2, 104–6
  managerial control, 85–7,
    104–13
  occupations, 32
  output growth, 33
  see also ownership; division of
    labour

radio
  industry trends, 40–1
  see also division of labour
Ray, L., 5
Reich, R., 9
reflexive production, 9
Ritzer, G., 6
Roberston, R., 162
Robinson, S., 97
Rogers, C., 19
Rothenbuhler, E., 35, 61
Royal Opera House, 48, 50n, 89

Saundry, R., 50n
Scannell, P., 28
Schlesinger, P., 167
scientific management, 5–6, 12, 14,
  17, 19, 96
  see also managerialism

Scott, A., 165
skills
  craft, 53, 59
  in creative industries, 16, 28–9
  standardization, 14–15, 26
small business, 8, 32, 37, 43, 75,
  139, 146, 148
Smith, C., 24, 150
Srebernby-Mohammadi, A., 162
Straw, W., 35
subsidy, 25, 30–1, 71
  see also Arts Council, National
    Lottery, performing arts,
    Royal Opera House

Taylor, F., 5, 129
teamwork, 3, 46, 68, 92, 117–19, 140
technology, *see* information
  technology
television,
  independent production, 58, 121
  industry trends, 38–40, 163
  managerial control, 113–26
  output, 38, 50n
  quotas, 39
  see also BBC, broadcasting,
    division of labour
theatre, *see* performing arts
Thompson, J., 24
trade unions, 17, 53, 130, 143
traditional organization, 99–100,
  113, 123–4, 153–4
Tunstall, J., 27, 39, 58
Twiss, B., 18

UNESCO, 150
Ursell, G., 148

Varlaam, C., 59

Weber, M., 4, 96, 112, 129